CONFIDENTIAL　　　A. E. F. No. 1040
　　　　　　　　　　　　G-5.

MANUAL

OF

EQUIPMENT

FOR

MACHINE GUN COMPANIES

HOTCHKISS MACHINE GUN MODEL 1914
SAINT-ÉTIENNE TRIPOD MODEL 1915
HOTCHKISS TRIPOD MODEL 1916
GUN CART MODEL 1907
AMMUNITION CART MODEL 1907

Ordnance Dept., May, 1918.　　　*Automatic Arms Division.*

The Naval & Military Press Ltd

Published by

The Naval & Military Press Ltd
Unit 5 Riverside, Brambleside
Bellbrook Industrial Estate
Uckfield, East Sussex
TN22 1QQ England

Tel: +44 (0)1825 749494

www.naval-military-press.com
www.nmarchive.com

In reprinting in facsimile from the original, any imperfections are inevitably reproduced and the quality may fall short of modern type and cartographic standards.

General Headquarters, A. E. F., France.
May 1918.

This manual with both English and French nomenclature is published for guidance of Machine Gun Company commanders, and Ordnance Officers in equipping and ordering parts for Machine Gun Companies.

TABLE OF CONTENTS

Pages.
- 3   Machine Gun organization per Division and Army Corps.
- 4   Issue of Indirect Fire Control Instruments, Hotchkiss M. G. Cos.
- 6   Issue of Equipment, Hotchkiss Machine Gun Companies.
- 8   Anti-Aircraft Machine Guns and Equipment for Balloon companies.
- 8   Machine Guns and Equipment for light Tanks (Renault).
- 8   Anti Aircraft Machine Guns and Equipment for protection of depots, hospitals, ammunition dumps, etc.
- 9   Anti-Aircraft Machine Guns and Equipment for heavy artillery and railroad artillery.
- 10   Nomenclature of Hotchkiss Machine Gun Model 1914 (Numerical arrangement).
- 13   Nomenclature of Hotchkiss Machine Gun Model 1914 (Group arrangement).
- 15   Spare Part Case No. 1 (Contents) Hotchkiss M. G.
- 17   Spare Part Case No. 2 (Contents) Hotchkiss M. G.
- 18   Gunner's Pouch (Contents).
- 18   Cleaning Kit (Contents).
- 18   Nomenclature of St-Étienne Tripod Model 1915 (Part numbers).
- 22   Nomenclature of St-Étienne Tripod Model 1915 (Group arrangement).
- 23   Nomenclature of Hotchkiss Tripod Model 1916 (Part numbers).
- 26   Nomenclature of Hotchkiss Tripod Model 1916 (Group arrangement).
- 32   Vertical Fire Bracket.
- 34   Machine Gun Cart Model 1907.
- 39   Machine Gun Cart Model 1907 — Accessories carried.
- 40   Ammunition Cart Model 1907.
- 45   Ammunition Cart Model 1907 — Accessories carried
- 46   Harness-French type 1861.
- 49   Head Harness-French type 1874.
- 49   French Supply Caisson.
- 49   Ammunition.
- 49   Horse Equipment.
- 50   Accessories.
- 51   Cartridges carried on light Carts.
- 51   Weight of Hotchkiss equipment.
- 52   General description of the Hotchkiss M. G. Model 1914.
- 53   Action of the mechanism of the Hotchkiss M. G. model 1914.
- 54   To strip the Hotchkiss Machine Gun.
- 55   To assemble the Hotchkiss Machine Gun.
- 56   Timing table (explaining action of the parts of the gun during one cycle).
- 62   Precautions to be taken before, during, and after firing Hotchkiss M. G.
- 63   Loading the Hotchkiss Machine Gun.
- 64   To Unload the Hotchkiss M. G.
- 64   To let down mechanism.
- 64   Jams, Malfunctions, Stoppages-Hotchkiss Machine Gun.

PLATES

	Pages.
I and II. — Hotchkiss Machine Gun	11-12
III an IV. — St-Étienne Tripod Model 1915	19-20
V, VI and VII. — Machine Gun Cart	36 to 38
VIII and IX. — Ammunition Cart	41-42
X. — Vertic l Fire Bracket	33
XI, XII, XIII and XIV. — Hotchkiss Tripod Model 1916	27 to 30
XV. — Harness-French type 1861	47
XVI. — Head Harness-French type 1874	48

M. G. ORGANIZATION PER DIVISION

4 Inf. M. G. Companies.
2 Brigade Battalions of 4 Companies each.
1 Divisional Battalion of 2 Companies motorized.
Total 14 M. G. Companies per Division.

ARMY CORPS

Each Army Corps (6 div.) has an Army Corps M. G. Battalion of 4 Companies, organized same as Inf. M. G. Companies for Anti-aircraft.

Issue of Indirect Fire control Instru

	M. G. COMPANY			BRIG. M. G. BATTA	
	Active.	Spare.	Total.	Active.	Spare.
Plotting board and tripod	—	—	4	—	—
Alidades	—	—	4	—	—
Declinators	—	—	4	—	—
Protractors	—	—	12	—	—
Reglettes	—	—	4	—	—
Zinc squares	—	—	4	—	—
Zinc scales	—	—	4	—	—
Canvas carrying case	—	—	4	—	—
Goniometer and tripod	—	—	2	—	—
Clinometers discontinued to Hotchkiss M. G. Co's.	—	—	—	—	—
Prismatic comp. and tripod	—	—	6	—	—
Levels	12	4	16	48	16
Indirect fire tables	24	8	32	96	32
Range finders	—	—	1	—	—
Trajectory Graphs 1/10000 horiz. 1/2000 vert.	—	—	12	—	—
Loading tools	—	—	—	—	—
Cases dispatch	—	—	6	—	—
Anemometer (*)	—	—	1	—	—
Barometer (*)	—	—	1	—	—
Periscope	—	—	4	—	—
Swivel cleaning rods	—	—	4	—	—
Thermometers	—	—	1	—	—
Elevating wheel Blocks	24	8	32	96	32
Traversing wheel Blocks	24	8	32	96	32
Crocus cloth (Quires)	—	—	2	—	—
Emery cloth (Quires)	—	—	2	—	—
Canton flannel (meters)	—	—	25	—	—
Blacksmith tools (**)	—	—	1	—	—

(*) Provisional Issue.
(**) Field Kit consisting of : 1 Clinch Cutter, 1 Clinch Iron, 1 Shoeing Knife.

ments, Hotchkiss M. G. Companies.

LION 4 COS. Total.	DIV. Art. Brig. A. A.	DIV. M. G. Ba. 2 Cos. Mot.	DIV.	ARMY CORPS TROOPS INF. M. G.			
				4 Cos. A. A. Mot.	Field Art. 12 Batt. A. A.	Field Heavy Art. A. A.	
16	—	8	56	16	—		
16	—	8	56	16	—		
16	—	8	56	16	—		
48	—	24	168	48	—		
16	—	8	56	16	—		
16	—	8	56	16	—		
16	—	8	56	16	—		
16	—	8	56	16	—		
8	—	4	28	8	—		
—	—	—	—	—	—		
24	—	12	84	24	—		
64	—	32	224	64	—		
128	72	64	520	128	48		No Indirect Fire Instruments required.
4	—	2	14	4	—		
48	—	24	204	48	24		
—	—	—	—	—	—		
24	—	12	84	24	—		
4	—	2	14	4	—		
4	—	2	14	4	—		
16	—	8	56	16	—		
16	18	8	74	16	12		
4	—	2	14	4	—		
128	—	64	448	128	—		
128	—	64	448	128	—		
8	5	4	33	8	24		
8	5	4	33	8	24		
100	60	50	410	100	50		
4	—	—	12	—	—		

1 Shoeing Hammer 10 oz., 1 Rasp 16″, 1 Hoof and Cutting Nippers,

Issue of Equipment, Hotchkiss M. G. Companies.

	MACHINE GUN COMPANY			BRIG. M. G. BA. 4 COS.			DIV. Art. Brig. A. A.	DIV. M. G. Ba. 2 Cos. Motorized.	DIVISION.	CORPS TROOPS.		Heavy Art.	
										Inf. M. G. 4 Cos. A. A. Mot.	Field Art. 12 Batt. A. A.	1 A. A. M. G. per Batt., all others, 2 A. A. M. G. per Battery.	Railway mounted
	Active.	Spare.	Total.	Active.	Spare.	Total.							
Hotchkiss Machine Gun.	12	4	16	48	16	64	36	32	260	64	24	24	—
Spare barrels	24	8	32	96	32	128	18	64	466	128	48	48	—
Tripod	12	4	16	48	16	64	36	32	260	64	24	24	—
Gunner's Pouch	12	4	16	48	16	64	36	32	260	64	24	24	—
Cleaning Kit (*)	4	—	4	—	16	16	36	32	116	64	24	—	—
Spare Part Case No. 1	6	2	8	24	8	32	9	16	121	32	12	—	—
Spare Part Case No. 2	6	2	8	24	8	32	9	16	121	32	12	—	—
Gun Cart	12	—	12	48	—	48	—	—	144	—	—	—	—
Ammunition Cart	12	—	12	48	—	48	—	—	144	—	—	—	—
Hotchkiss Anti - Avion Mounts	4	—	4	16	—	16	36	8	92	48	24	—	—
Hotchkiss Anti - Avion Sights	4	—	4	16	—	16	36	8	92	48	24	—	—
Emergency Mounts (473.55/100)	—	—	—	—	—	—	—	—	—	—	—	—	—
Combat Wagons (4 horse)	12	—	12	8	—	8	—	—	24	—	—	—	—
Belt boxes	2	—	2	144	—	144	216	72	720	144	144	144	—
Belts (250 rounds)	36	—	36	144	—	144	216	72	720	144	144	144	—
Strip boxes	36	—	36	912	—	912	216	456	3408	912	144	144	—
Strips	228	—	2736	10944	—	10944	2592	5472	40896	10944	1728	—	—

(*) Cleaning kit to contain : 1 pr. chain mittens, 1 chain shoulder strap, 1 canvas water bucket, 1 oil can, cleaning rags. Ammunition cart accessory : Extra kits issued to Companies not receiving carts.

	BRIG. M. G. Bat. 4 Cos.	DIVISION.

Blacksmith tools to Bn. Headquarters Co. . . . .
Consisting of :
    Anvil, 34 pounds.
    Apron, blacksmiths.
    Box shoeing leather.
    Chisel, cold iron.
    Clinch cutter.
    Clinching iron.
    Creaser, steel handle.
    File, 12 in. second cut.
    File, 8 in. 3 square taper.
    Fire Rake.
    Fire Shovel.
    Hammers.
      Rounding, 2 lb., 14 in. handle
      Shoeing 10 oz.
    Handles, cold chisel, spare.
    Hardie, 9/16" shank 1" bit.
    Nipper, cutting 14".
    Pritchel, 9/16" flats, 9".
    Schaller forge.
    Tool kit for Schaller forge.
    Schaller forge tool chest.
    Shoeing knife.
    Shoeing pincers, 14".
    Shoeing rasp 16".
    Tongs, horseshoer's 18.5 oz.
    Vise 2.5" jaws.
    Whetstone, 10".
    Wrench, screw, 8 in.
	1	2

Anti-Aircraft Machine Guns and Equipment for Balloon Companies.

Six Machine Guns per company. Three companies per section

For each company :

    6 Hotchkiss machine guns, cal. 8 mm.
    6 tripods, model 1915.
    6 gunners pouch.
    6 cleaning kit.
    3 spare parts case No. 1.
    3 spare parts case No. 2.
    3 spare barrels.
    6 anti-avion mounts.
    6 anti-avion sighs.
    2 cleaning rods, swiveled.
  72 strip boxes.
864 strips.
20736 rounds 8 mm. ammunition.

Machine Guns and Equipment for Light Tanks (Renault).

   1 Hotchkiss machine gud, cal. 8 mm.
   1 gunners pouch.
   1 cleaning kit.
   1 spare parts case (*).
   1 spare barrel.
  50 belt boxes.
  50 belts, metal (96 rounds).
4800 rounds 8 mm. ammunition.

Anti-Aircraft Machine Guns and Equipment for Protection of Depots, Hospitals, Ammunition Dumps, etc.

1 Hotchkiss machine gun, caliber 8 mm.
1 tripod.
1 gunners pouch.
1 cleaning kit.

(*) 1 spare parts case No. 1, and 1 spare parts case No. 2, with each two guns issued.

1 spare parts case No. 1 (*).
1 spare parts case No. 2 (*).
1 spare barrel (for every two guns).
1 anti-avion mount.
1 anti-avion sight.
6 belt boxes
6 belts (250).
6 strip boxes (12 strips).
72 strips (24 rounds).
3228 rounds of 8 mm. ammunition.

Anti-Aircraft Machine Guns and Equipment for Heavy artillery and Railroad artillery.

For each battery.

R. R. Art.	Heavy Art.	
1	2	Hotchkiss machine guns, cal. 8 mm.
1	2	tripods.
1	2	gunners pouch.
1	2	cleaning kit.
1	1	spare parts case No. 1 (**).
	1	spares parts case No. 2 (**).
1	1	spare barrels.
1	2	Anti-avion mounts.
1	2	anti-avion sights.
6	12	belt boxes.
6	12	belts.
6	12	strip boxes (12 strips).
72	144	strips (24 rounds).
3228	6456	rounds, 8 mm. ammunition.

(*) 1 spare parts case No. 1, and 1 spare parts case No. 2, for each two guns issued.
(**) Spare parts case No. 1 or No. 2.

Numerical Nomenclature of Hotchkiss Machine Gun Model 1914.

(Plates I and II.)

Part Nos.		
1	Barrel.	Canon.
4	Barrel stop pins (2).	Butées du canon (2).
5	Front sight band.	Frette porte-guidon.
6	Gas cylinder band.	Frette support.
7	Radiator.	Radiateur.
8	Barrel lock.	Clavette du canon.
8a	Barrel lock collar.	Bague de clavette du canon.
8b	Cotter pin.	Goupille de clavette du canon.
9	Gas cylinder locking screw.	Vis de fixation du cylindre à gaz.
10	Gas cylinder.	Cylindre à gaz.
12	Gas regulator.	Régulateur.
16	Receiver.	Boîte de culasse.
16a	Receiver recoil blocks (2).	Coins d'appui (2).
16b	Receiver recoil block pin.	Goupille de coin d'appui.
18	Rear sight complete.	Hausse complète.
18a	Rear sight bed.	Pied de hausse.
18b	Rear sight bed spring.	Ressort de hausse.
18c	Rear sight bed spring screw.	Vis du ressort de hausse.
18d	Rear sight leaf.	Planche de hausse.
18e	Rear sight leaf pin.	Axe de planche de hausse.
18f	Rear sight slide.	Curseur de hausse.
18g	Rear sight slide plungers (2).	Verrou de curseur de hausse (2).
18h	Rear sight slide plunger springs (2).	Ressort de verrou de curseur de hausse (2).
26	Elevating gear trunnion cap.	Chape d'attache de vis de pointage.
29	Feed box.	Couloir d'alimentation.
32	Feed box locking pin.	Clavette du couloir d'alimentation.
33	Piston.	Piston.
49	Breech block.	Culasse mobile nue.
50	Locking dog.	Verrou de fermeture.
53	Striker.	Percuteur.
54	Extractor.	Extracteu .
55	Extractor spring.	Ressort d'extracteur.
56	Ejector.	Éjecteur.
57	Sear.	Détente.
60	Sear spring.	Ressort de détente.
61	Feed ratchet pin	Arbre du mécanisme d'alimentation.

Part Nos.

62	Feed wheel.	Entraîneur.
65	Safety sear.	Arrêtoir.
69	Safety sear spring.	Ressort d'arrêtoir.
70	Feed ratchet pawl.	Cliquet.
74	Feed ratchet pin spring.	Ressort de cliquet
75	Return spring.	Ressort de rappel
76	Handle block.	Couvre-culasse.
77	Return spring guide.	Verrou de broche de couvre-culasse.
77a	Return spring guide pin.	Goupille d'arrêt du verrou de broche de couvre-culasse.
78	Handle block pin.	Broche de couvre-culasse.
79	Pistol grip.	Pistolet.
80	Deflector.	Déflecteur.
80a	Deflector rubber buffer.	Tampon en caoutchouc pour déflecteur.
81	Cocking piece.	Levier d'armement.
82	Cocking piece spring latch.	Ressort d'accrochage du levier d'armement.
83	Piston stop plug.	Butée du piston.
86	Front sight.	Guidon.
96	Connecting link pin.	Broche d'attache.
96a	Connecting link pin plunger and cotter pin.	Goupille de clef de broche d'attache. Goupille fendue de la goupille de clef de broche d'attache.
96b	Connecting link pin plunger spring.	Ressort de clef de broche d'attache.
97	Connecting link.	Chape intermédiaire.
118	Feed strip.	Bande rigide.
119	Metal belt.	Bande articulée.

Group Nomenclature of the Hotchkiss Machine Gun Model 1914.

(Plates I and II.)

Barrel Group.

1	Barrel.	Canon.
86	Front sight.	Guidon.
5	Front sight band.	Frette porte-guidon.
7	Radiator.	Radiateur.
4	Barrel stop pins (2).	Butées du canon (2).
6	Gas cylinder band.	Frette support.
10	Gas cylinder.	Cylindre à gaz.
12	Gas regulator.	Régulateur.
9	Gas cylinder locking screw.	Vis de fixation du cylindre à gaz.

Feed Mechanism Group.

Part Nos.		
29	Feed box.	Couloir d'alimentation.
32	Feed box locking pin.	Clavette du couloir d'alimentation.
65	Safety sear.	Arrêtoir.
69	Safety sear spring.	Ressort d'arrêtoir.
62	Feed wheel.	Entraîneur.
61	Feed ratchet pin.	Arbre du mécanisme d'alimentation.
70	Feed ratchet pawl.	Cliquet.
74	Feed ratchet pin spring.	Ressort de cliquet.
80	Deflector.	Déflecteur.
80a	Deflector rubber buffers.	Tampon en caoutchouc pour déflecteur.

Receiver Group.

16	Receiver.	Boîte de culasse.
76	Handle block.	Couvre-culasse.
78	Handle block pin.	Broche de couvre-culasse.
77	Return spring guide.	Verrou de broche de couvre-culasse.
77a	Return spring guide pin.	Goupille d'arrêt du verrou de broche de couvre-culasse.
79	Pistol grip.	Pistolet.
56	Ejector.	Éjecteur.
81	Cocking piece.	Levier d'armement.
82	Cocking piece spring latch.	Ressort d'accrochage du levier d'armement.
16a	Receiver recoil blocks, 1 pr.	Coin d'appui.
16b	Receiver recoil block pins (2).	Goupille de coin d'appui.
83	Piston stop plug.	Butée du piston.
8	Barrel lock.	Clavette du canon.
8a	Barrel lock collar.	Bague de clavette du canon.
8b	Barrel lock cotter pin.	Goupille de clavette du canon.
97	Connecting link.	Chape intermédiaire.
96	Connecting link pin.	Broche d'attache.
96a	Connecting link pin plunger.	Goupille de clef de broche d'attache.
96b	Connecting link pin spring.	Ressort de clef de broche d'attache.
96c	Connecting link pin cotter pin.	Goupille fendue de la goupille de clef de broche d'attache.
26	Elevating gear trunnion cap.	Chape d'attache de vis de pointage.

Rear Sight Group.

Part Nos.		
18a	Bed.	Pied de hausse.
18b	Bed spring.	Ressort de hausse.
18c	Bed spring screw.	Vis du ressort de hausse.
18d	Leaf.	Planche de hausse.
18e	Leaf pin.	Axe de planche de hausse.
18f	Slide.	Curseur de hausse.
18g	Slide plungers (2).	Verrou de curseur de hausse.
18h	Slide plunger springs (2).	Ressort de verrou de curseur de hausse.

Firing Mechanism Group.

75	Return spring.	Ressort de rappel.
33	Piston.	Piston.
49	Breech block.	Culasse mobile nue.
50	Locking dog.	Verrou de fermeture.
53	Striker.	Percuteur.
54	Extractor.	Extracteur.
55	Extractor spring.	Ressort d'extracteur.

Trigger Group.

57	Sear.	Détente.
60	Sear spring.	Ressort de détente.

Hotchkiss Automatic Machine Gun
Spare Part Case No 1.

Sacoche (grande) (N° 1) (en cuir).

Part Nos.	No. Pièces.		
9	1	Locking screw gas cylinder.	Vis de fixation du cylindre à gaz.
49	1	Breech block complete.	Culasse mobile complète.
		Breech block case, leather.	Étui pour culasse mobile, en cuir.
53	1	Striker.	Percuteur.
54	2	Extractors.	Extracteur.
55	2	Extractor springs.	Ressort d'extracteur.
56	1	Ejector.	Éjecteur.
57	1	Sear.	Détente.
60	1	Sear spring.	Ressort de détente.
65	1	Safety sear.	Arrêtoir.
69	1	Safety sear spring.	Ressort d'arrêtoir.

Part Nos.	Nos. Pièces.		
74	1	Feed ratchet pin spring	Ressort de cliquet.
75	1	Return spring.	Ressort de rappel.
80a	2	Deflector rubber buffers.	Tampon en cauoutchouc pour déflecteur.
96	1	Connecting link pin.	Broche d'attache.
96a	1	Connecting link pin plunger.	Goupille de clef de broche d'attache.
96b	1	Connecting link pin spring.	Ressort de clef de broche d'attache.
96c	1.	Connecting link pin cotter pin.	Goupille fendue de la goupille de. clef de broche d'attache.
97	1	Connecting link.	Chape intermédiaire.
	1	Traversing clamp.	M choires (paire).
	1	Traversing clamp lever.	Levier de débrayage.
	1	Traversing clamp spring.	Ressort de mâchoires.
	1	Barrel cleaning rod, 2 sections.	Hamped'écouvillon en deux pièces (pour le canon).
	1	Gas cylinder cleaning rod, 2 sections.	Écouvillon pour cylindre à gaz en deux pièces.
	1	Scraper for gas cylinder.	Grattoir pour le cylindre.
	12	Cleaning brushes (barrel).	Brosses à le canon.
	1	Hammer, model 1880.	Marteau modèle 1880.
	1	Barrel wrench.	Clef modèle 1908 pour le canon.
	1	Screw driver.	Tournevis emmanché.
	1	File.	Lime douce plate emmanchée.
	1	Chamber gauge.	Vérificateur de feuillure.
	1	Hand extractor.	Crochet éjecteur.
	1	Oil can.	Burette à huile.
	1	Grease box full.	Boîte à graisse garnie.
	1	Manual 1917 for '14 H. M. G.	Aide-mémoire pour mitrailleuse H.
	1	Box, zinc, and cover of canvas, containing spare parts.	Boîte prismatique en zinc pour rechanges d'affût-trépied.

Contents of zinc box of tripod spare parts :

    1 Arm lock handle spring.
    1 Arm lock handle spring locking bolt.
   10 Pins assorted.
    1 Cotter pin.
    5 Rivets.
    1 Elevating block trunnion lock.
    1 Elevating block trunnion lock spring.
    1 Elevating block locking pin.
    1 Knee joint lock plunger.
    1 Knee joint lock spring.
    1 Telescopic elevating screw hook lock.

1 Telescopic elevating screw hook spring.
1 Trunnion cap lock.
1 Trunnion cap lock spring.
1 Trunnion cap lock spring plug screw.
1 Trunnion cap wing nut.
1 Trunnion cap case locking nut.
1 Upper leg head joint pin.
1 Upper leg head joint pin collar.
1 Upper leg head joint pin collar pin.

Spare Part Case No 2 (Leather).

Sacoche (grande) (N° 2) (en cuir).

Part Nos.	No. Pieces		
9	1	Gas cylinder locking screw.	Vis de fixation du cylindre à gaz.
33	1	Piston.	Piston.
53	1	Striker.	Percuteur.
54	2	Extractors.	Extracteurs.
55	2	Extractor springs.	Ressort d'extracteur.
56	1	Ejector.	Éjecteur.
57	1	Sear.	Détente.
60	1	Sear spring.	Ressort de détente.
65	1	Safety sear.	Arrêtoir.
69	1	Safety sear spring.	Ressort d'arrêtoir.
74	1	Feed ratchet pin spring	Ressort de cliquet.
75	1	Return spring.	Ressort de rappel.
80a	2	Deflector rubber buffers.	Tampons en caoutchouc pour déflecteur.
96	1	Connecting link pin.	Broche d'attache.
96a	1	Connecting link pin plunger.	Goupille de clef de broche d'attache.
96b	1	Connecting link pin spring.	Ressort de clef de broche d'attache.
96c	1	Connecting link pin cotter pin.	Goupille fendue de la goupille de clef de broche d'attache.
	1	Cleaning rod, barrel, 2 sections.	Hampe d'écouvillon pour le canon, en deux pièces.
	1	Cleaning rod, gas cylinder 2 sections.	Écouvillon du cylindre à gaz en deux pièces.
	12	Cleaning brushes (barrel).	Brosses à canon.
	1	Scraper for gas cylinder.	Grattoir pour le cylindre.
	1	Hand extractor.	Crochet éjecteur.
	1	Hammer, model 1880.	Marteau modèle 1880.
	1	Screw driver.	Tournevis emmanché.
	1	Barrel wrench.	Clef de démontage modèle 1908 pour le canon.

No. Pieces	
1 File.	Lime douce plate emmanchée.
1 Grease box full.	Boîte à graisse garnie.
1 Oil can.	Burette à huile.
1 Front sight cover.	Couvre-guidon.
1 Tripod wrench.	Clef de démontage de l'affût.
2 Traversing stops.	Butoir de fauchage en direction.
3 Elevating wheel blocks.	Butoir de fauchage en hauteur.

Gunners Pouch.
Sacoche petite.

1. Extractor.	Extracteur.
1 Extractor spring.	Ressort d'extracteur.
1 Striker.	Percuteur.
1 Brush, varnish.	Pinceau à graisse.
1 Defective cartridge extractor.	Tire-douille modèle 1907.
1 Hand extractor.	Crochet éjecteur.
1 Wrench for gas regulator.	Clef pour l'affût et le régulateur.
1 Oil can.	Huilier en laiton.

Cleaning Kit.
Sac à chiffons.

1 Pair chain mittens.	Paire de gants spéciaux servant à manipuler le canon lorsqu'il est chaud.
1 Chain shoulder strap.	Épaulière.
1 Canvas water bucket.	Seau en toile.
1 Oil can.	Burette à huile.
Cleaning rags.	Chiffons, 1 kilo.

SAINT-ÉTIENNE TRIPOD MODEL 1915.

Numerical Nomenclature of Parts.

(Plates III and IV.)

Part Nos.		
1	Traversing head.	Support pivotant.
3	Trunnion cap case.	Boîte à sus-bande.
3a	Trunnion cap case nut.	Écrou de la boîte à sus-bande.
3b	Rotating trunnion lock.	Sus-bande à rotation avec axe (droite et gauche).

Hotchkiss Machine Gun

Full view, left han

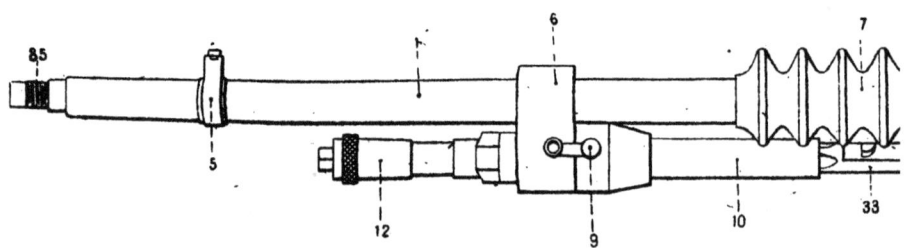

Full top vie

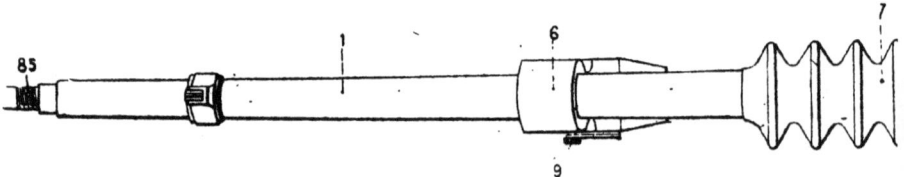

a Model 1914

Pl. I.

d side.

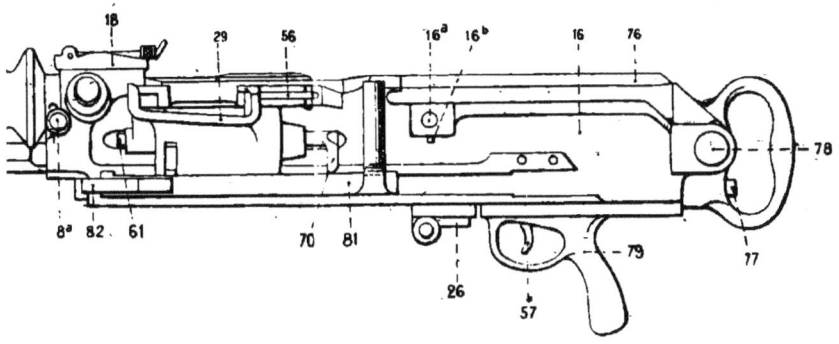

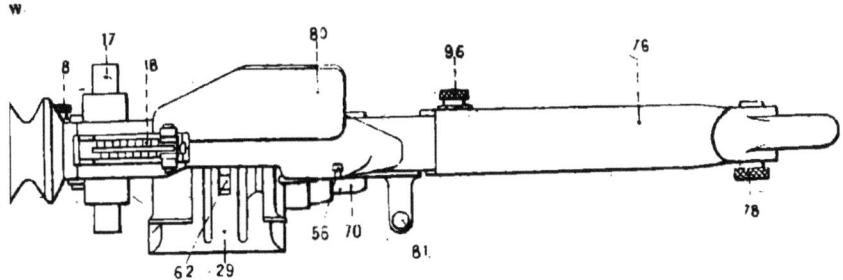

Hotchkiss Machine Gu

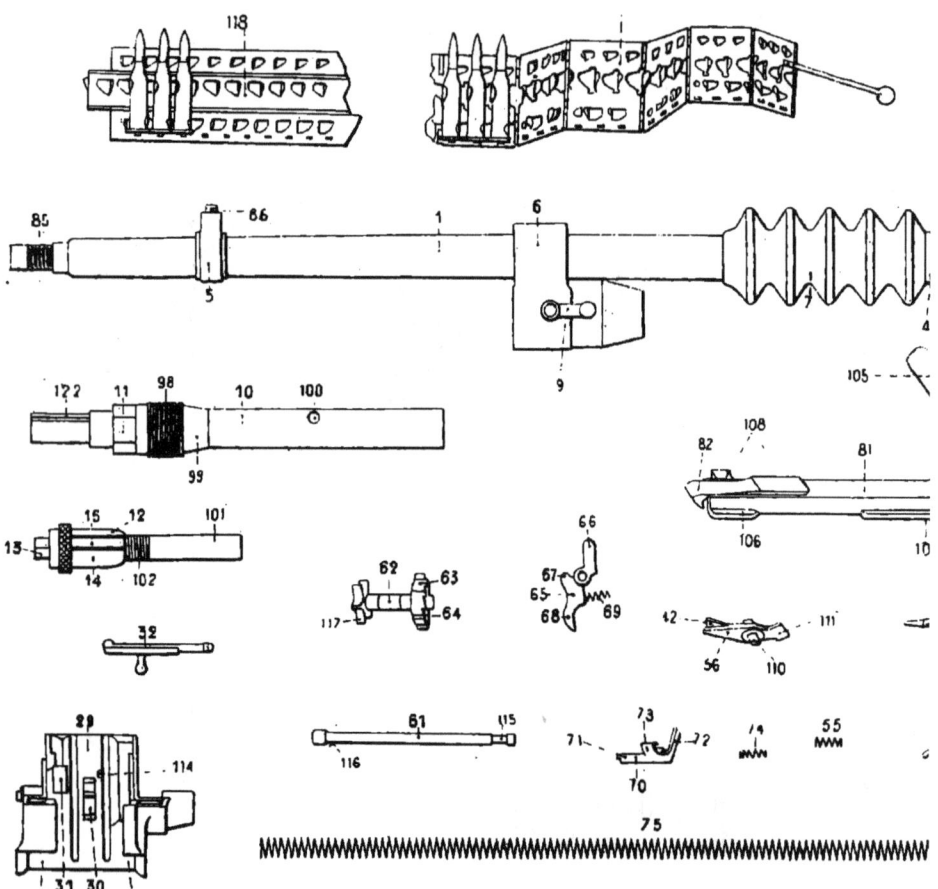

Pl. II.

n Model 1914 stripped.

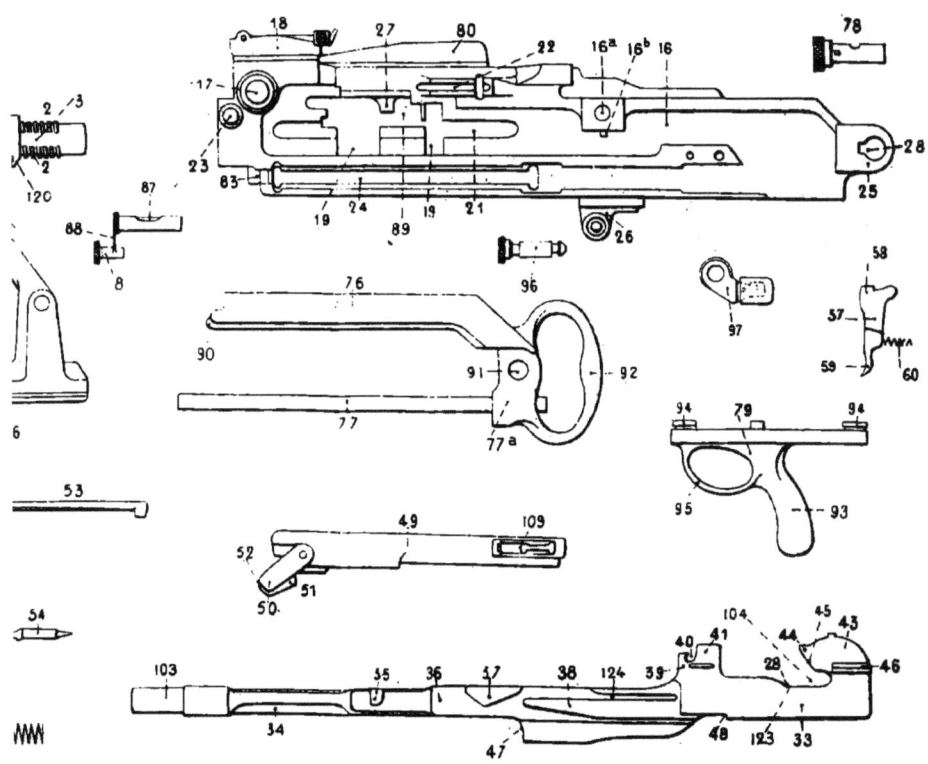

Pl. III.

**Omnibus Tripod
Saint-Étienne Model 1915.**

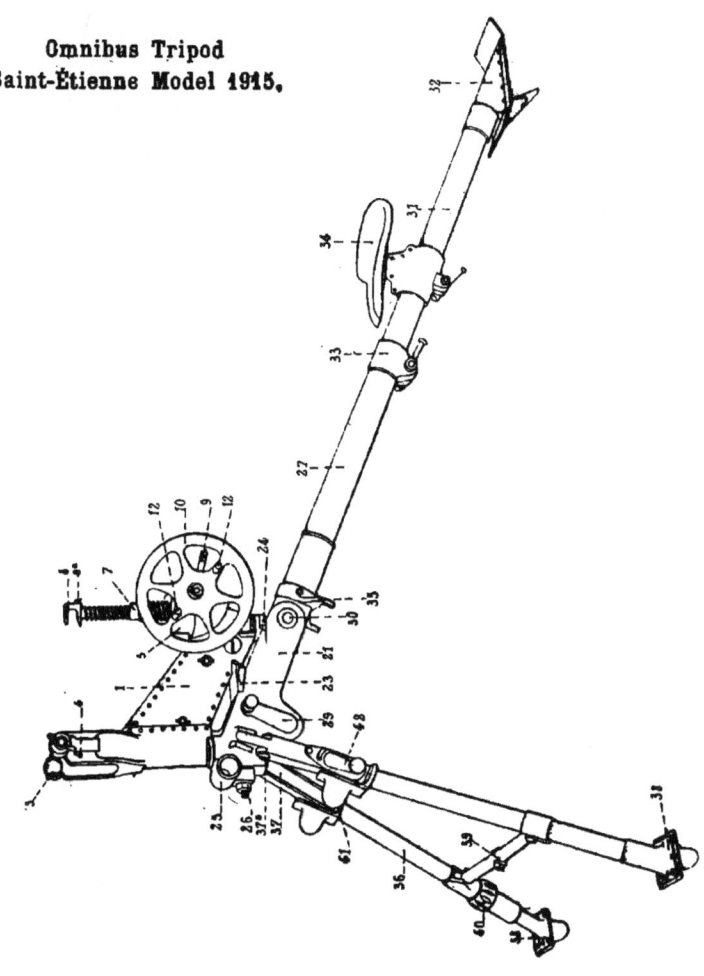

Pl. IV.   — 20 —

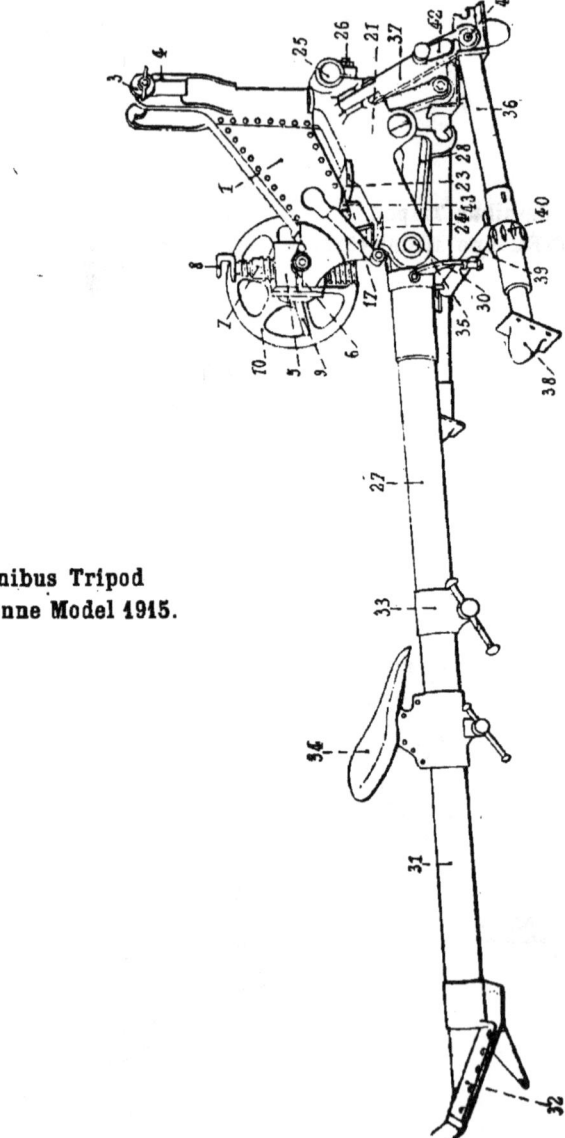

Omnibus Tripod
St-Étienne Model 1915.

Part Nos.		
3c	Rotating trunnion lock wing nut.	Écrou à oreilles des sus-bandes à rotation.
4	Trunnion cap spring lock	Levier-arrêtoir de sus-bande à rotation avec axe, poussoir, ressort et vis-bouchon
4a	Trunnion cap lock spring.	Ressort à boudin du levier arrêtoir de sus-bande.
4b	Trunnion cap lock spring retaining screw.	Vis-bouchon du ressort à boudin du levier arrêtoir de sus-bande.
5	Elevating gear split nut.	Boîte à tourillons.
6	Elevating gear trunnion caps (2).	Sus-bande de boîte à tourillons.
7	Elevating screw (brass).	Vis de pointage (laiton).
8	Elevating screw (steel).	Vis de pointage (acier).
8a	Elevating screw hook lock.	Arrêtoir à levier avec axe et ressort.
8b	Elevating screw hook spring.	Ressort de l'arrêtoir à levier.
8c	Elevating screw hook pin.	Goupille axe de l'arrêtoir à levier.
9	Elevating wheel index.	Index du volant de pointage en hauteur.
9a	Elevating wheel index screw.	Vis de l'index du volant de pointage en hauteur.
9b	Elevating wheel index key.	Cran d'arrêt de l'index.
10	Elevating wheel.	Volant de pointage.
10a	Elevating wheel shaft nut.	Écrou de l'axe du volant de pointage.
12	Elevating wheel finger holds (2).	Tenons de manœuvre du volant de pointage.
12a	Elevating wheel finger hold axis pins (2).	Goupille du tenon de manœuvre.
17	Traversing clamp lever.	Levier de débrayage.
21	Pivot body.	Corps de pivot avec circulaire.
23	Knurled arc.	Secteur strié.
24	Circular support.	Circulaire solidaire du corps de pivot.
25	Carrying bar socket.	Douille fendue.
26	Carrying bar socket clamp nut.	Écrou de serrage de douille.
27	Trail.	Flèche télescopique.
28	Arm.	Bras antérieur.
29	Arm lock.	Manivelle d'arrêt de la position de flèche.
30	Trail joint bolt.	Boulon d'accouplement de la flèche.
30a	Trail joint bolt nut.	Écrou du boulon d'accouplement de la flèche.
31	Inner trail tube.	Rallonge de flèche.

Part Nos.		
32	Inner trail tube shoe.	Semelle de flèche.
33	Trail clamp.	Collier fendu de flèche.
33a	Trail clamp hand bolt.	Boulon à manette.
33b	Trail clamp hand bolt turning bar.	Levier de serrage du boulon à manette.
34	Seat.	Siège.
34a	Seat clamp.	Collier de serrage de siège.
34b	Seat clamp hand bolt.	Boulon à manette.
34c	Seat clamp hand bolt turning bar.	Levier de serrage du boulon à manette.
36	Fore legs (2).	Montant de pied antérieur.
37	Fore leg head (right)(1).	Tête de montant (droite).
37	Fore leg head (left) (1).	Tête de montant (gauche).
37a	Fore-leg head joint axis.	Axe d'accouplement de montant.
38	Fore leg shoes (2).	Semelle à ergot de montant de pied antérieur.
39	Separators (2).	Compas.
40	Leg leveling screw.	Écrou moleté de pied antérieur.
41	Knee joints (2).	Genouillère.
41a	Knee joint pin.	Cheville de la genouillère.
41b	Knee joint nut.	Écrou de la genouillère.
42	Knee joint locks (2).	Manivelle de genouillère avec axe, bouton, écrou et goupille.
43	Index finger.	Index de repérage en direction.
44	Traverse graduated dial	Limbe gradué pour repérage en direction.

Group Nomenclature of Parts.

(Plates III and IV.)

Traversing Group.

1	Traversing head.	Support pivotant.
3	Trunnion cap case.	Boîte à sus-bande.
4	Trunnion cap spring lock	Levier arrêtoir de sus-bande.
5	Elevating gear split nut.	Boîte à tourillons.
6	Elevating gear trunnion caps (2).	Susbande de boîte à tourillons.
7	Elevating screw (brass).	Vis de pointage (laiton).
8	Elevating screw (steel).	Vis de pointage (acier).
9	Elevating wheel index.	Index du volant de pointage.
10	Elevating wheel.	Volant de pointage.
12	Elevating wheel finger holds (2).	Tenons de manœuvre du volant de pointage.
17	Traversing clamp lever.	Levier de débrayage.

Part Nos.		
48	Index finger.	Index de repérage en direction.

Tripod.

21	Pivot body.	Corps de pivot avec circulaire.
23	Knurled arc.	Secteur strié.
24	Circular support.	Circulaire solidaire du corps de pivot.
25	Carrying bar socket.	Douille fendue.
26	Carrying bar socket clamp nut.	Écrou de serrage de douille.
27	Trail.	Flèche.
28	Arm.	Bras antérieur.
29	Arm lock.	Manivelle d'arrêt de la position de flèche.
30	Trail joint bolt.	Boulon d'accouplement de la flèche.
31	Inner trail tube.	Rallonge de flèche.
32	Inner trail tube shoe.	Semelle de flèche.
33	Trail clamp.	Collier fendu de flèche.
34	Seat.	Siège.
36	Fore legs (2).	Montant de pied antérieur.
37	Fore leg heads (2).	Tête de montant.
38	Fore leg shoes (2).	Semelle à ergot de montant de pied antérieur.
39	Separators (2).	Compas.
40	Leg leveling screw.	Écrou moleté de pied antérieur.
41	Knee joints (2).	Genouillère.
42	Knee joint locks (2).	Manivelle de genouillère avec axe, bouton, écrou et goupille.
44	Traverse graduated dial.	Limbe gradué pour repérage en direction.

HOTCHKISS TRIPOD MODEL 1916.

Numerical Nomenclature of Parts.

(Plates XI, XII, III and XIV.)

1	Double ended front leg axis.	Axe à chapes des pieds antérieurs.
2	Traversing clamp lever axis.	Axe excentrique du levier de blocage.
3	Cam lever axis.	Axe porte-cames.
4	Traversing clamp lever handle axis.	Axe-rivet de la poignée du levier de blocage.

Part Nos.

5	Traversing clamp lever collar.	Bague-arrêtoir du levier de blocage.
6	Trunnion slide stop pin (not shown).	Bonhomme de sus-bande.
7	Fore leg axis.	Boulon-axe de pied antérieur.
8	Elevating clamp bolt.	Boulon de blocage en hauteur.
9	Trail tube.	Bras antérieur de la flèche télescopique.
10	Traversing stop guide.	Butée de pivotement.
11	Traversing stop (right).	Butoir de fauchage en direction (droite).
12	Traversing stop (left).	Butoir de fauchage en direction (gauche).
13	Lower elevating screw clamp.	Butoir de fauchage en hauteur (inférieur).
14	Upper elevating screw clamp.	Butoir de fauchage en hauteur (supérieur).
15	Traversing brake shoe (not shown).	Cale de blocage.
16	Left cam.	Came gauche du levier à cames.
16a	Right cam.	Came droite du levier à cames
17	Traversing thumb stop.	Cliquet de butoir de fauchage en direction.
18	Trail clamp.	Collier de serrage de bras antérieur de flèche.
19	Seat clamp.	Collier de serrage de siège.
20	Pivot body.	Corps de pivot.
21	Hand wheel nut for elevating screw.	Douille-écrou du boulon de blocage.
22	Trail nut with pin.	Douille-écrou du collier de serrage du bras antérieur de flèche avec manette.
23	Seat nut with pin.	Douille-écrou du collier de serrage de siège avec manette.
24	Elevating screw nut.	Douille de vis de pointage en hauteur.
25	Traversing head assembling nut.	Écrou d'assemblage du support pivotant.
26	Hand wheel nut pin.	Ergot-arrêtoir de douille-écrou du boulon de blocage.
27	Hand wheel nut stop.	Ergot-butée de douille-écrou de boulon de blocage.
28	Eccentric roller (not shown).	Galet.
29	Traversing thumb stop axis.	Goupille-axe de cliquet.
30	Pin for double ended front leg axis.	Goupille de l'axe à chapes.

Part Nos.		
31	Traversing clamp lever collar pin.	Goupille de bague-arrêtoir.
32	Left cam pin (not shown).	Goupille de came gauche.
33	1 mm. cotter pin for elevating screw clamp (not shown).	Goupille fendue de 1 mm., butoir de fauchage en hauteur.
34	1 mm. 5 cotter pin for seat clamp (not shown).	Goupille fendue de 1 mm. 5, douille du collier de siège.
35	2 mm. cotter pin for trail clamp (not shown).	Goupille fendue de 2 mm., douille du collier de flèche.
36	3 mm. cotter pin for fore leg axis, traversing lever, and trunnion cap.	Goupille fendue de 3 mm., boulon-axe des pieds antérieurs, levier de blocage, sus-bande.
37	6 mm. cotter pin for assembling nut (not shown).	Goupille fendue de 6 mm., écrou d'assemblage.
38	Cam lever.	Levier à cames.
39	Traversing clamp lever.	Levier de blocage.
40	Fore leg (right).	Pied antérieur (droite).
41	Fore leg (left).	Pied antérieur (gauche).
42	Pivot (not shown).	Pivot.
43	Traversing lever handle.	Poignée du levier de blocage.
44	Trail tube male.	Rallonge de flèche.
45	Trunnion slide stop spring (not shown).	Ressort de bonhomme.
46	Traversing thumb stop spring (not shown).	Ressort de cliquet.
47	Cam lever spring (not shown).	Ressort de levier à cames.
48	Fore leg axis collar (not shown).	Rondelle de boulon-axe de pied antérieur.
49	Brass elevating clamp bolt washer (not shown).	Rondelle de boulon de blocage.
50	Seat.	Siège du tireur.
51	Traversing head.	Support pivotant.
52	Sliding trunnion cap (right).	Sus-bande à tiroir (droite).
53	Sliding trunnion cap (left).	Sus-bande à tiroir (gauche).
54	Screws for traversing guide (not shown).	Vis de butée de pivotement.
55	Shoulder screws for traversing brake shoe (not shown).	Vis de cale de blocage.
56	Upper and lower clamping screws and pins.	Vis de collier de butoir en hauteur (supérieur et inférieur).
57	Trail clamp screw.	Vis de collier de serrage de flèche.

Part Nos.		
58	Seat clamp screw.	Vis de collier de serrage de siège.
59	Elevating steel screw with eye.	Vis de pointage en hauteur avec anneau (acier).
60	Brass elevating screw with handle.	Vis-écrou de pointage en hauteur avec volant.

Group Nomenclature of Parts.

(Plates XI, XII, XIII and XIV.)

Traversing Group.

2	Traversing clamp lever axis.	Axe excentrique du levier de blocage.
4	Traversing clamp lever handle axis.	Axe-rivet de la poignée du levier de blocage.
5	Traversing clamp lever collar.	Bague-arrêtoir du levier de blocage.
6	Trunnion slide stop pin (not shown).	Bonhomme de sus-bande.
8	Elevating clamp bolt.	Boulon de blocage en hauteur.
10	Traversing stop guide.	Butée de pivotement.
11	Traversing stop (right).	Butoir de fauchage en direction (droite).
12	Traversing stop (left).	Butoir de fauchage en direction (gauche).
13	Lower elevating screw clamp.	Butoir de fauchage en hauteur (inférieur).
14	Upper elevating screw clamp.	Butoir de fauchage en hauteur (supérieur).
15	Traversing brake shoe (not shown).	Cale de blocage.
17	Traversing thumb stop.	Cliquet de butoir de fauchage en direction.
21	Hand wheel nut for elevating screw.	Douille-écrou du boulon de blocage.
24	Elevating screw nut.	Douille de vis de pointage en hauteur.
26	Hand wheel nut pin.	Ergot-arrêtoir de douille-écrou du boulon de blocage.
27	Hand wheel nut stop.	Ergot-butée de douille-écrou de boulon de blocage.
28	Eccentric roller (not shown).	Galet.
29	Traversing thumb stop axis.	Goupille-axe de cliquet.

— 27 —

Pl. XI.

Hotchkiss Tripod Model 1916.
With vertical fire bracket.

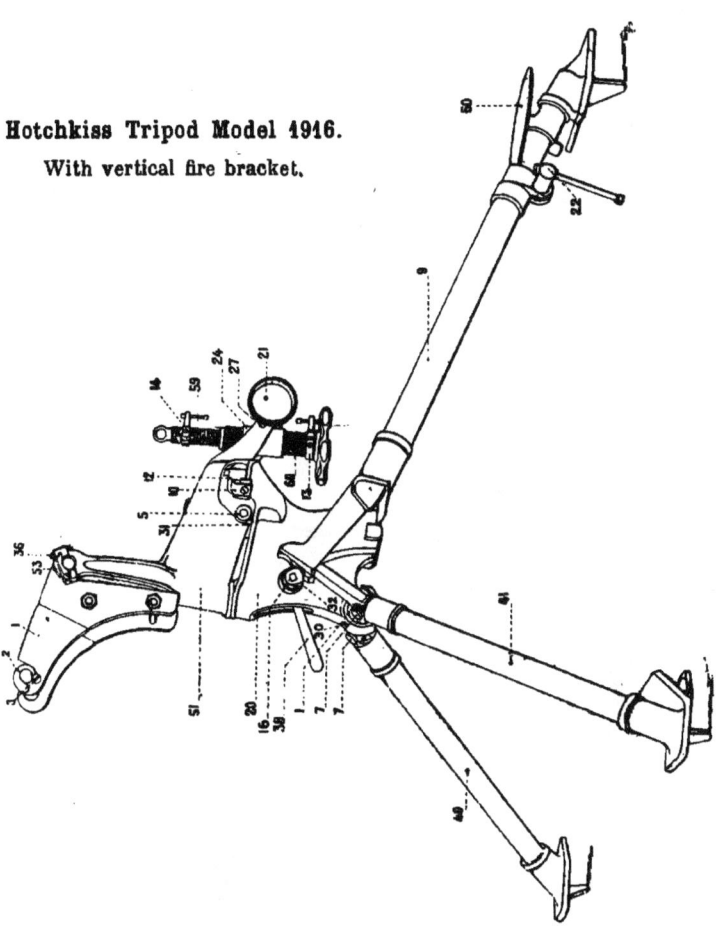

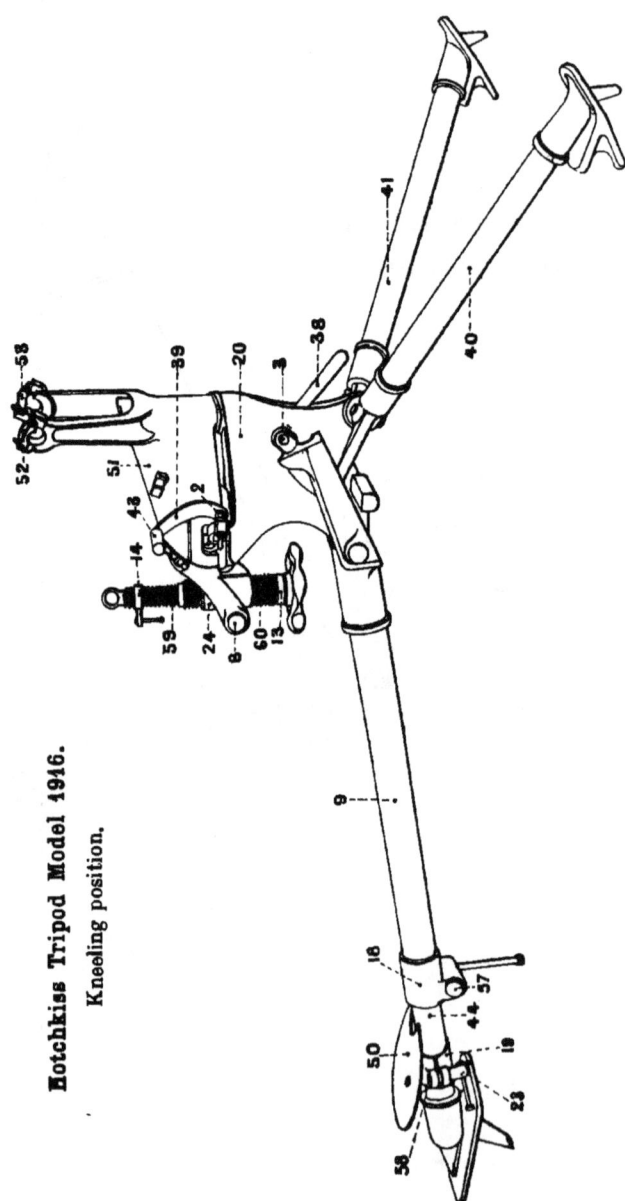

Pl. XII. — 28 —

Hotchkiss Tripod Model 1916.
Kneeling position.

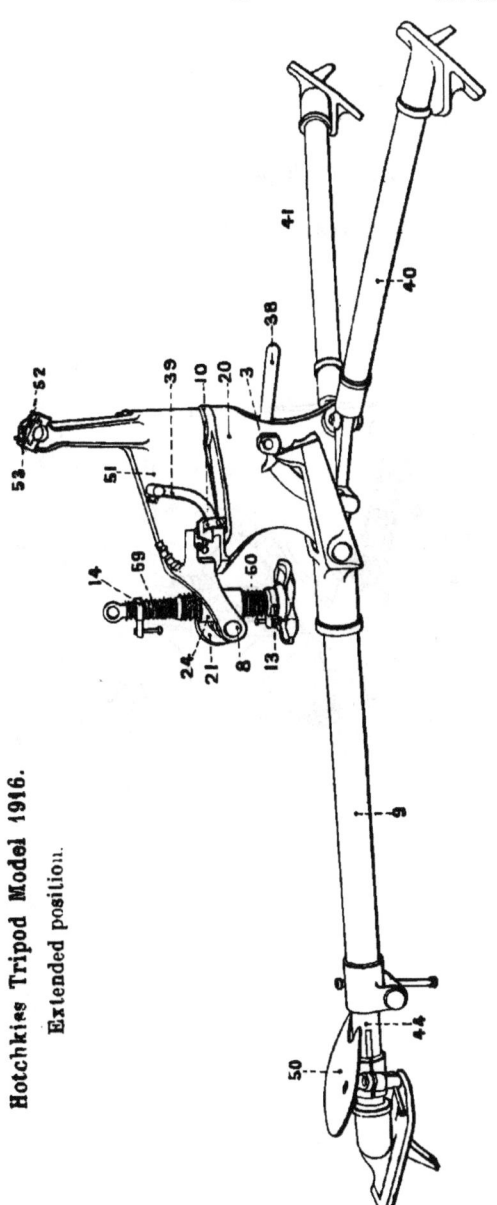

Hotchkiss Tripod Model 1916.
Extended position.

Pl. XIV.

Hotchkiss Tripod Model 1916.

Showing traversing and elevating mechanism.

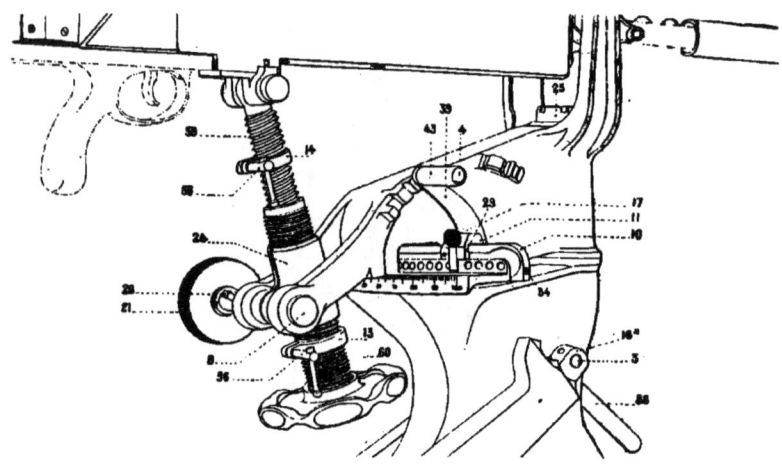

— 31 —

Part Nos.		
31	Traversing clamp lever collar pin.	Goupille de bague-arrêtoir.
33	1 mm. cotter pin for elevating screw clamp (not shown).	Goupille fendue de 1 mm., butoir de fauchage en hauteur.
36	3 mm. cotter pin for traversing lever and trunnion cap.	Goupille fendue de 3 mm., levier de blocage, sus-bande.
39	Traversing clamp lever.	Levier de blocage.
43	Traversing lever handle.	Poignée du levier de blocage.
45	Trunnion slide stop spring (not shown).	Ressort de bonhomme.
46	Traversing thumb stop spring (not shown).	Ressort de cliquet.
49	Brass elevating clamp bolt washer (not shown).	Rondelle de boulon de blocage.
51	Traversing head.	Support pivotant.
52	Sliding trunnion cap (right).	Sus-bande à tiroir (droite).
53	Sliding trunnion cap (left).	Sus-bande à tiroir (gauche).
54	Screws for traversing guide (not shown).	Vis de butée de pivotement.
55	Shoulder screws for traversing brake shoe (not shown).	Vis de cale de blocage.
56	Upper and lower clamping screws and pins.	Vis de collier de butoir en hauteur (supérieur et inférieur).
59	Elevating steel screw with eye.	Vis de pointage en hauteur avec anneau (acier).
60	Brass elevating screw with handle.	Vis-écrou de pointage en hauteur avec volant.

Tripod Group.

1	Double ended front leg axis.	Axe à chapes des pieds antérieurs.
3	Cam lever axis.	Axe porte-cames.
7	Fore leg axis.	Boulon-axe de pied antérieur.
9	Trail tube.	Bras antérieur de la flèche télescopique.
16	Left cam.	Came gauche du levier à cames.
16a	Right cam.	Came droite du levier à cames.
18	Trail clamp.	Collier de serrage de bras antérieur de flèche.
19	Seat clamp.	Collier de serrage de siège.

Part Nos.		
20	Pivot body	Corps de pivot.
22	Trail nut with pin.	Douille-écrou du collier de serrage du bras antérieur de flèche avec manette.
23	Seat nut with pin.	Douille-écrou du collier de serrage de siège avec manette.
25	Traversing head assembling nut.	Écrou d'assemblage du support pivotant.
30	Pin for double ended front leg axis.	Goupille de l'axe à chapes.
32	Left cam pin (not shown).	Goupille de came gauche.
34	1 mm. 5 cotter pin for seat clamp (not shown).	Goupille fendue de 1 mm. 5, douille du collier de siège
35	2 mm. cotter pin for trail clamp (not shown).	Goupille fendue de 2 mm., douille du collier de flèche.
36	3 mm. cotter pin for fore leg axis.	Goupille fendue de 3 mm., boulon-axe des pieds antérieurs.
37	6 mm. cotter pin for assembling nut (not shown).	Goupille fendue de 6 mm., écrou d'assemblage.
38	Cam lever.	Levier à cames.
40	Fore leg (right).	Pied antérieur (droite).
41	Fore leg (left).	Pied antérieur (gauche).
42	Pivot (not shown).	Pivot.
44	Trail tube male.	Rallonge de flèche.
47	Cam lever spring (not shown).	Ressort de levier à cames.
48	Fore leg axis collar (not shown).	Rondelle de boulon-axe de pied antérieur.
50	Seat.	Siège de tireur.
57	Trail clamp screw.	Vis de collier de serrage de flèche.
58	Seat clamp screw.	Vis de collier de serrage de siège.

VERTICAL FIRE BRACKET.

Support pour le tir vertical.

(Plate X.)

1	Vertical fire side plates (right and left).	Flasques (droite et gauche) du support pour le tir vertical.
2	Trunnion lock.	Sus-bande de support pour le tir vertical.
3	Trunnion lock screw.	Vis de sus-bande de support pour le tir vertical.

Pl. X.

Vertical Fire Bracket.

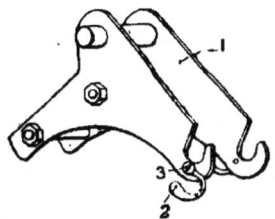

Vertical Fire Bracket as issued to Infantry Machine Gun Companies.

Note. — This Vertical Fire Bracket is made for facilitating the firing under high angles of machine gun free from the elevating screw.

It may be used on all tripod mounts, 1907-1915 St-Étienne, 1914 and 1916 Hotchkiss.

For use, mount the bracket on the tripod vertically by means of its trunnions. Turn it opposite to the traversing head. Lock the trunnion caps of the mount. Place the machine gun on the mount, the barrel directed towards the trail, and lock trunnions of the bracket.

For placing the Hotchkiss Machine gun, be careful to bring the gun almost horizontal in order to avoid being hindered by the feed box.

The Vertical Fire Bracket may be transported on the Gun Cart.

MACHINE GUN CART.

Voiturette porte-mitrailleuse.

(Plates V, VI and VII.)

Part Nos.		
1	Shaft frame (right and left).	Armature de brancard (droite et gauche).
2	Hand draught frame.	Armature de tirage.
3	Hand draught crossbar.	Bâton de remorque.
4	Movable shaft.	Brancard mobile.
4a	Movable shaft (articulated).	Brancard mobile (articulé).
5	Movable shaft stop pin with chain.	Clavette-arrêtoir de brancard mobile avec chaînette.
6	Hand draught pole stop pin with chain.	Clavette-arrêtoir de bâton de remorque avec chaînette.
7	Loading straps.	Courroies de chargement.
8	Drag hooks.	Crochets de trait.
9	Axle.	Essieu.
9a	Pin for ring at axle end.	Clavette à anneau de bout d'essieu.
10	Shaft clamp.	Étrier de brancard.
11	Draught pole.	Flèche de tirage.
12	Outer side pieces.	Longerons extérieurs.
13	Inner side pieces.	Longerons intérieurs.
14	Singletree eye.	Œil de palonnier.
15	Singletree.	Palonnier.
16	Loading shelves.	Planchettes de chargement.
17	Handles.	Poignées.
18	No. 5 A Wheel.	Roue N° 5 A.
19	Pole props.	Servante.

Part Nos.		
20	Hand draught pole.	Timon de remorque.
21	Splinter bar.	Volée.
22	Wooden block for tripod mount.	Billot en bois pour affût-trépied.
23	Metal case for accessories.	Caissette métallique à accessoires.
	Spare horse shoes.	Ferrure de rechange.
	Horse shoe nails (1 pkg.).	Clous à ferrer (1 paquet).
	Frost nails.	Crampons à glace.
	Tap wrench.	Clef à taraud.
	Nail wrench.	Clef à pointe.
	Instruction pamphlets.	Livre d'instruction.
	Pair chain mittens.	Paire de gants spéciaux.
	Chain shoulder strap.	Épaulière.
	Oil can.	Burette à huile.
	Canvas water bucket.	Seau en toile.
	Rags.	Chiffons, 1 kilo.
	Whip.	Fouet.
24	M. G. Ammunition chest.	Casier à munitions pour voiturette porte-mitrailleuse.
26	Lashing strap staple for camping outfit.	Chape d'attache de la courroie de brêlage de l'ustensile de campement.
27	Lashing rope staple.	Chape d'attache de corde de brêlage.
30	Traversing head case staple.	Chape d'attache de support pivotant.
32	Axe staple.	Chape de fixation pour hache.
33	Dragging bar pin with chain.	Chevillette de timon de remorque avec chaînette.
35	Tripod mount lashing strap.	Courroie de brêlage de l'affût.
36	Ammunition chest lashing strap.	Courroie de brêlage des caisses à munitions.
37	M. G. lashing strap.	Courroie de brêlage de la mitrailleuse.
38	M. G. rear support.	Porte-mitrailleuse de derrière, type omnibus.
39	Barrel fixing clamp.	Étrier porte-canon.
40	Tripod mount cap square rack.	Support à sus-bande pou affût-trépied.
41	M. G. front support.	Porte-mitrailleuse de devant, type omnibus.
42	Cross piece.	Traverse.
43	Stop peg for tool chest.	Verrou de fixation de la caissette à accessoires.
44	Tripod head mount with case or cover.	Étui pour affût-trépied avec support pivotant.
45	Ammunition chest and cover.	Caisse à munitions H. avec bâche.

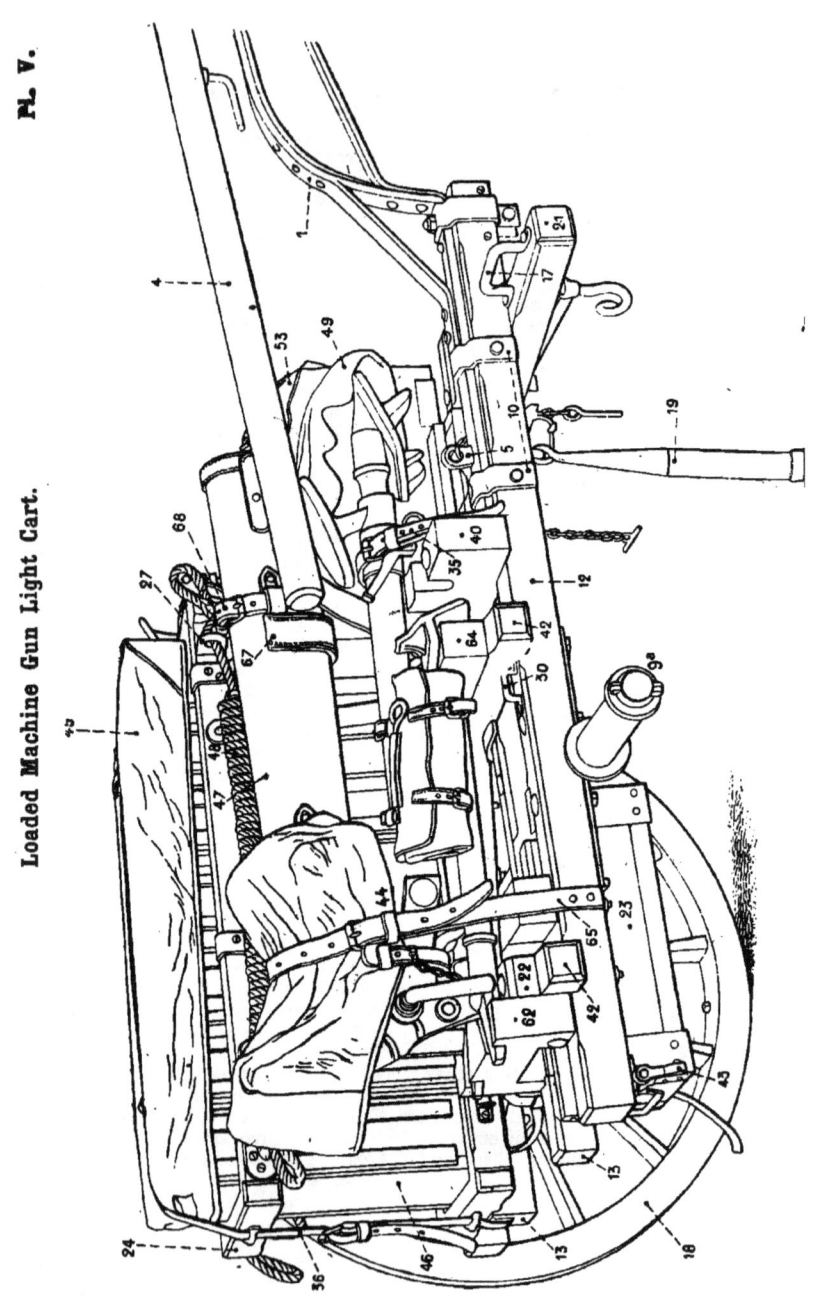

Pl. V.

Loaded Machine Gun Light Cart.

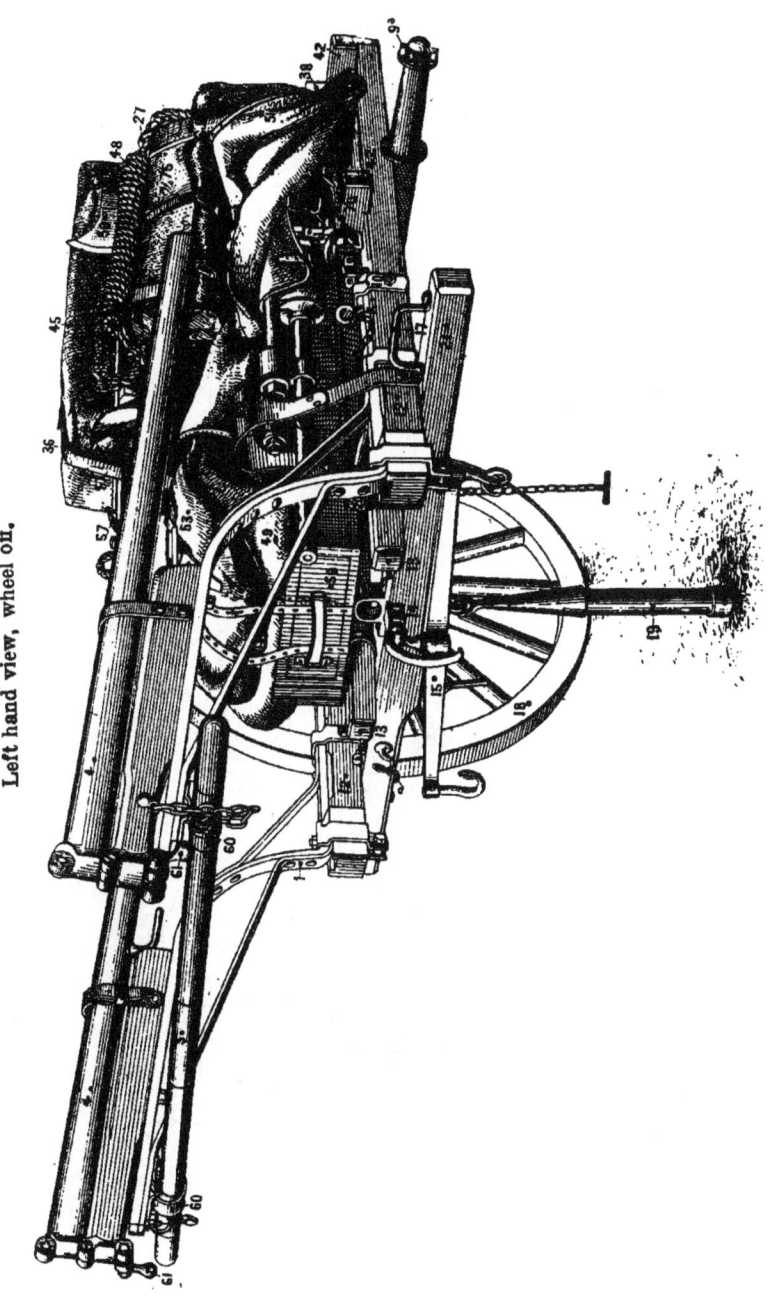

Pl. VI.

Loaded Machine Gun Light Cart.
Left hand view, wheel off.

Pl. VII.

Machine Gun Light Cart, unloaded.

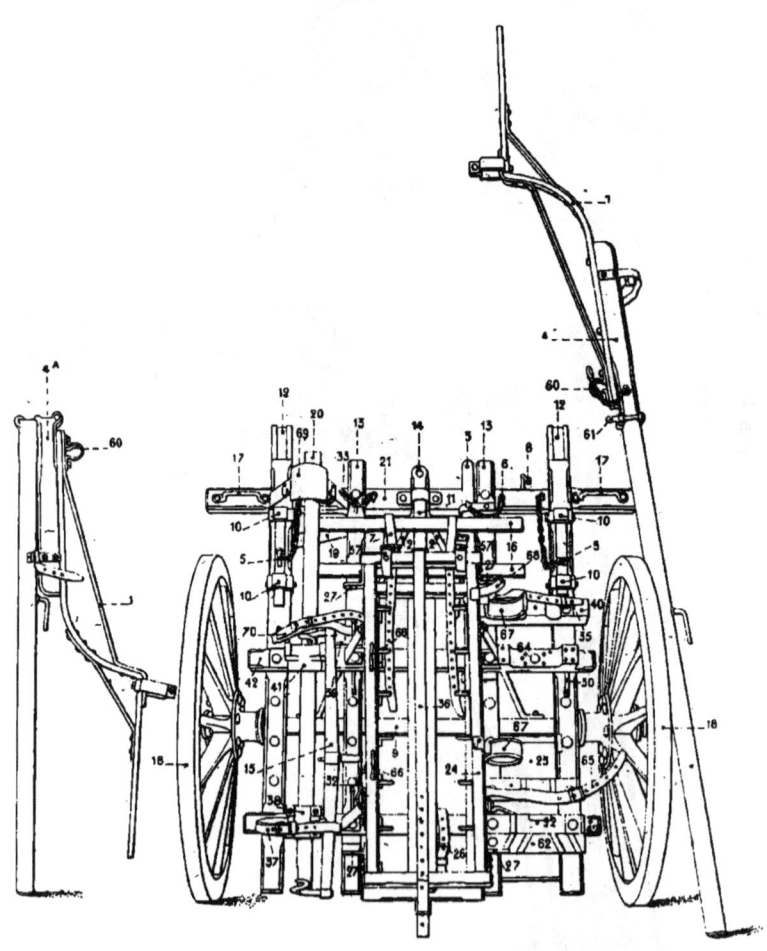

Part Nos.		
46	Ammunition chests for rigid strips.	Caisses à munitions H. pour bandes rigides.
47	Spare barrel case.	Étui de canon de rechange.
48	Lashing ropes (2).	Cordes de brêlage (2).
49	Horse blankets (2).	Couvertures de cheval (2).
50	Axe.	Hache.
51	Machine gun case.	Étui de mitrailleuse.
53	Rag bag.	Sac à chiffons.
54	Grooming bag (not shown).	Sac de pansage.
	Nose-bag (not shown).	Musette-mangeoire.
55	Camping kit (under cart).	Ustensile de campement.
57	Flash arrestor lashing strap.	Courroie de brêlage de cache-flammes.
58	Flash arrestor.	Cache-flammes.
59	Hotchkiss ammunition cases for belts.	Caisses à munitions Hotchkiss pour bandes articulées.
60	Dragging pole cross bar socket.	Chapes de traverse de timon de remorque.
61	Double hinge peg.	Chevillette de charnière double.
62	Hotchkiss mount rear rack.	Porte-affût H. de derrière, type omnibus.
64	Hotchkiss mount front rack.	Porte-affût H. de devant, type omnibus.
65	Hotchkiss mount lashing strap.	Courroie de brêlage du porte-affût de derrière (Hotchkiss).
66	Hotchkiss pouch staples (2).	Chape des courroies de brêlage de la grande sacoche Hotchkiss.
67	Hotchkiss barrel case supports (2).	Support d'étui de canon Hotchkiss.
68	Hotchkiss barrel case lashing strap.	Courroie de brêlage de l'étui à canon Hotchkiss.
69	Hotchkiss protecting support for M. G.	Support protecteur pour mitrailleuse H.
70	Lashing strap for front M. G. rack.	Courroie de brêlage du porte-mitrailleuse, de devant.
75	Large Hotchkiss pouch for spares.	Grande sacoche aux rechanges Hotchkiss.

Accessories Carried on Machine Gun Cart.

7	Ammunition cases (strips).	Caisses à munitions pour bandes rigides (7).
1	Ammunition case (belt).	Caisse à munitions pour bande articulée.
	Machine gun in case.	Mitrailleuse dans son étui.

Tripod mount with traversing head in case.	Affût Hotchkiss avec bâche de tête.
Spare barrel in case.	Canon de rechange dans son étui.
Spare part pouche.	Sacoche aux rechanges.
Gunner's pouch.	Sacoche petite.
Flash arrestor.	Cache-flammes.
Horse blankets (2).	Couvertures de cheval (2).
Surcingle.	Sous-ventrière.
Rag bag.	Sac à chiffons.
Grooming bag.	Sac de pansage.
Nose-bag.	Musette-mangeoire.
Lashing ropes (2).	Cordes de brêlage (2).
Portable axe.	Hache.
Camping kit.	Ustensile de campement.
Spare jointed shaft.	Brancard articulé de rechange.
Metal case for accessories	Caisse métallique à outils.
Spare horse shoes.	Ferrure de rechange.
Horse shoe nails (1 pkg.).	Clous à ferrer (1 paquet).
Frost nails.	Crampons à glace.
Tap wrench.	Clef à taraud.
Nail wrench.	Clef à pointe.
Instruction pamphlets.	Livres d'instruction.
Pair chain mittens.	Paire de gants spéciaux.
Chain shoulder strap.	Épaulière.
Oil can.	Burette à huile.
Water bucket, canvas.	Seau en toile.
Rags.	Chiffons, 1 kilo.
Whip.	Fouet.

AMMUNITION CART.

Voiturette porte-munitions.

(Plates VIII and IX.)

Part Nos.		
1	Shaft frame (right and left).	Armature de brancard (droite et gauche).
2	Hand draught frame.	Armature de tirage.
3	Hand draught cross bar.	Bâton de remorque.
4	Movable shaft.	Brancard mobile.
5	Movable shaft stop pin with chain.	Clavette-arrêtoir de brancard mobile avec chaînette.

Loaded Ammunition Light Cart.
Left hand view, wheel off.

— 42 —

Pl. IX.

Ammunition Light Cart, unloaded.
Bottom view.

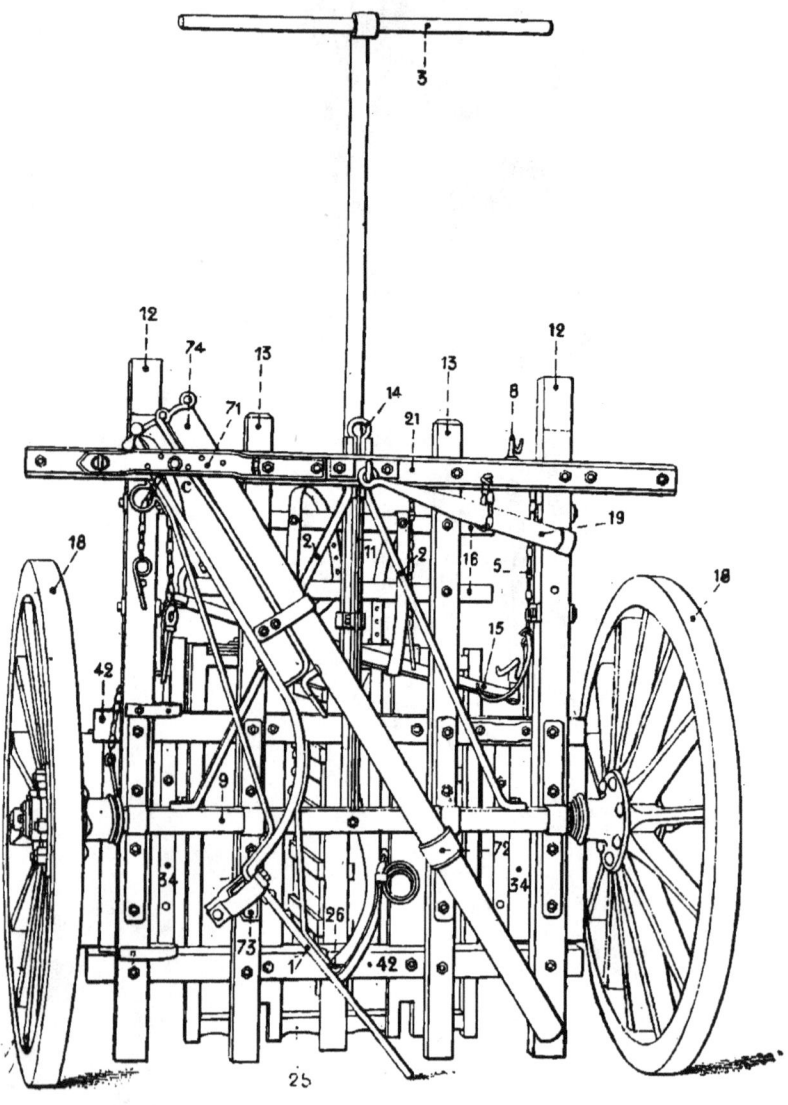

Part Nos.		
7	Loading straps.	Courroies de chargement.
8	Drag hooks.	Crochets de trait.
9	Axle.	Essieu.
9a	Pin for ring at axle end.	Clavette à anneau de bout d'essieu.
10	Shaft clamp.	Étrier de brancard.
11	Draught pole.	Flèche de tirage.
12	Outer side pieces.	Longerons extérieurs.
13	Inner side pieces.	Longerons intérieurs.
14	Singletree eye.	Œil de palonnier.
15	Singletree.	Palonnier.
16	Loading shelves.	Planchettes de chargement.
17	Handles.	Poignées.
18	No 5 A wheel.	Roue N° 5 A.
19	Pole props.	Servante.
20	Hand draught pole.	Timon de remorque.
21	Splinter bar.	Volée.
25	Ammunition chest for ammunition cart.	Casier à munitions pour voiturette porte-munitions.
26	Lashing strap staple for camping outfit.	Chape d'attache de la courroie de brêlage de l'ustensile de campement.
27	Lashing rope staple.	Chape d'attache de corde de brêlage.
33	Dragging bar pin with chain.	Chevillette de timon de remorque avec chaînette.
34	Tool chest No. 1.	Coffre à outils.
	Hand axes (2).	Hache à main (2).
	Spoke shave.	Plane à main pour rayon de roue.
	Nail wrenches (2).	Clefs à pointe (2).
	Tap wrench.	Clef à taraud.
	File, bastard.	Lime plate bâtarde de 25 cm.
	File, rat tail and handle 8 mm.	Lime en queue de rat avec manche, de 8 mm.
	Hand auger.	Vrille de 5 mm.
	Punches (2).	Poinçon (2).
	Chisel, cold.	Ciseau à froid.
	Bits assorted (3).	Mors assortis (3).
	Hammer.	Marteau de menuisier emmanché.
	Chisel, hand (2).	Ciseau à main (2).
	Saw.	Scie égoïne.
	2 Prs. mule shoes.	Fers à mulet (2 paires).
	1 Pkg. shoe nails.	Clous pour fers à mulet (1 paquet).
	Saddler's kit for harness repairs.	Un nécessaire de bourrelier pour les réparations aux harnais.
	Lamp.	Lanterne d'escouade.

Part Nos.		
34	Tool chest No. 2.	Coffre à outils N° 2.
	Wrench.	Clef.
	Bit stock.	Mèche à percer.
	Nail wrench.	Clef à pointe.
	Drills (3).	Mors (3).
	Screws (1 pkg.).	Vis (1 paquet).
	Screw driver.	Tournevis ordinaire emmanché de 4 mm.
	Set of Bolts (nuts, pins, wood screws, pins with small chains), 1 package	Jeu de boulons (écrous, goupilles, vis à bois, chevillettes avec chaînettes) 1 paquet.
	Chains with large pin (2).	Chaînes avec grandes goupilles (2).
	Chains with small pin (2).	Chaînes avec petites goupilles (2).
	Chain with fastener.	Chaîne avec agrafe.
	Large washers (4).	Rondelles (grandes) (4).
	Clamps (4).	Presses à main (4).
	Pin-setter.	Chasse-goupille de 0,006
	Washer, leather.	Rondelle de cuir gras.
	Washer for axle end.	Rondelle de bout d'essieu.
	Roll sheet iron.	Rouleau de tôle.
36	Ammunition chest lashing strap.	Courroie de brêlage des caisses à munitions.
42	Cross piece.	Traverse.
45	Ammunition chest, canvas case or cover.	Bâche de caisses à munitions.
48	Lashing ropes (2).	Cordes de brêlage (2).
49	Horse blankets (2).	Couvertures de cheval (2).
52	Range finder tripod case.	Étui de pied de télémètre.
54	Nose-bag (not shown).	Musette mangeoire.
	Grooming bag (not shown).	Sac de pansage.
59	Hotchkiss ammunition cases for belts.	Caisses à munitions Hotchkiss (pour bandes articulées).
60	Dragging pole cross bar socket.	Chapes de traverse de timon de remorque.
61	Double hinge peg.	Chevillette de charnière double.
71	Detachable metal fittings for spare shaft.	Armature métallique mobile pour brancard de rechange.
72	Socket for spare jointed shaft.	Douille pour le brancard articulé de rechange.
73	Flat hook for spare jointed shaft.	Crochet plat pour le brancard articulé de rechange.
74	Spare jointed shaft.	Brancard mobile de rechange (articulé).

Accessories Carried on Ammunition Cart.

12	Ammunition chests (strips).	Caisses à munitions pour bandes rigides.
2	Ammunition chests (belts).	Caisses à munitions pour bandes articulées.
1	Tool Chest No. 1.	Caisse à outils N° 1.
	Hand axes (2).	Hache à main (2).
	Spoke shave.	Plane à main pour rayon de roue.
	Nail wrenches (2).	Clefs à pointe (2).
	Tap wrench.	Clef à taraud.
	File, bastard.	Lime plate bâtarde de 25 cm.
	File, rat tail and handle 8 mm.	Lime en queue de rat avec manche, de 8 mm.
	Hand auger.	Vrille de 5 mm.
	Punches (2).	Poinçon (2).
	Chisel, cold.	Ciseau à froid.
	Bits assorted (3).	Mors assortis (3).
	Hammer.	Marteau de menuisier emmanché.
	Chisel, hand (2).	Ciseau à main (2).
	Saw.	Scie égoïne.
	2 Prs. mule shoes.	Fers à mulet (2 paires).
	1 Pkg. shoe nails.	Clous pour fers à mulet (1 paquet).
	Saddler's kit for harness repairs.	Un nécessaire de bourrelier pour les réparations aux harnais.
	Lamp.	Lanterne d'escouade.
1	Tool Chest No. 2.	Caisse à outils N° 2.
	Wrench.	Clef.
	Bit stock.	Mèche à percer.
	Nail wrench.	Clef à pointe.
	Drills (3).	Mors (3).
	Screws (1 pkg.).	Vis (1 paquet).
	Screw driver.	Tournevis ordinaire emmanché de 4 mm.
	Set of Bolts (nuts, pins, wood screws, pins with small chains) 1 pkg.	Jeu de boulons (écrous, goupilles, vis à bois, chevillettes avec chaînettes) 1 paquet.
	Chains with large pin (2).	Chaînes avec grandes goupilles (2).
	Chains with small pin (2).	Chaînes avec petites goupilles (2).
	Chain with fastener.	Chaîne avec agrafe.
	Large washers (4).	Rondelles (grandes) (4).
	Clamps (4).	Presses à main (4).

Pin-setter.	Chasse - goupille de 6 mm.
Washer, leather.	Rondelle de cuir gras.
Washer for axle end.	Rondelle de bout d'essieu.
Roll sheet iron.	Rouleau de tôle.
Grease box.	Boîte à graisse.
Lashing rope (2).	Cordes de brêlage (2).
Range finder & tripod in case.	Télémètre et pied dans son étui.
Horse blanket.	Couverture de cheval.
Surcingle.	Sous-ventrière.
Grooming bag.	Sac de pansage.
Nose-bag.	Musette mangeoire.
Spare jointed shaft.	Brancard de rechange.
Spare linch pin.	Esse de rechange.

Harness for Draft Animals.

The Harness of the Draft Animals of The Machine Gun and Ammunition Light Carts is made up of complete sets of Harness type 1861, with Head Harness type 1874.

This type of harness is used to lead by hand or in exceptional cases by reins; horses are lead in Infantry Machine Gun units.

Harness.

(French type 1861.)

Part Letters.

A.	Dutch collar.	Dessus de cou.
B.	Rein rings.	Anneaux de rênes.
C.	Check rein hook.	Crochet de rêne.
D.	Saddle.	Sellette.
E.	Thill loop.	Boucle de brancard.
F.	Back strap.	Surdos.
G.	Hold back strap.	Courroie de reculement.
H.	Hip strap.	Bras du haut d'avaloire.
I.	Crupper strap.	Courroie de croupière.
J.	Breeching ring.	Boucle d'avaloire.
K.	Crupper (proper).	Croupière.
L.	Breeching suspender strap.	Branche.
M.	Breeching body.	Avaloire.
N.	Thill strap.	Courroie porte-brancard.
O.	Trace chain.	Chaîne de bout de trait.
P.	Trace rope.	Rallonge de trait.
Q.	Trace.	Trait.
R.	Cincha.	Sangle.
S.	Belly band.	Sous-ventrière.
T.	Breast band.	Bricole.

Pl. XV.

Harness Type 1861.

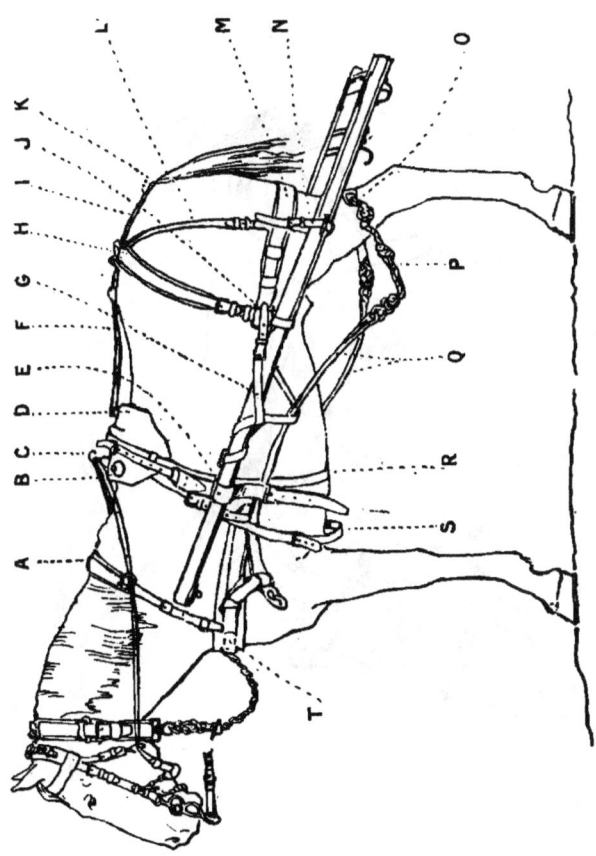

Pl. XVI.

Head Harness Type 1874.

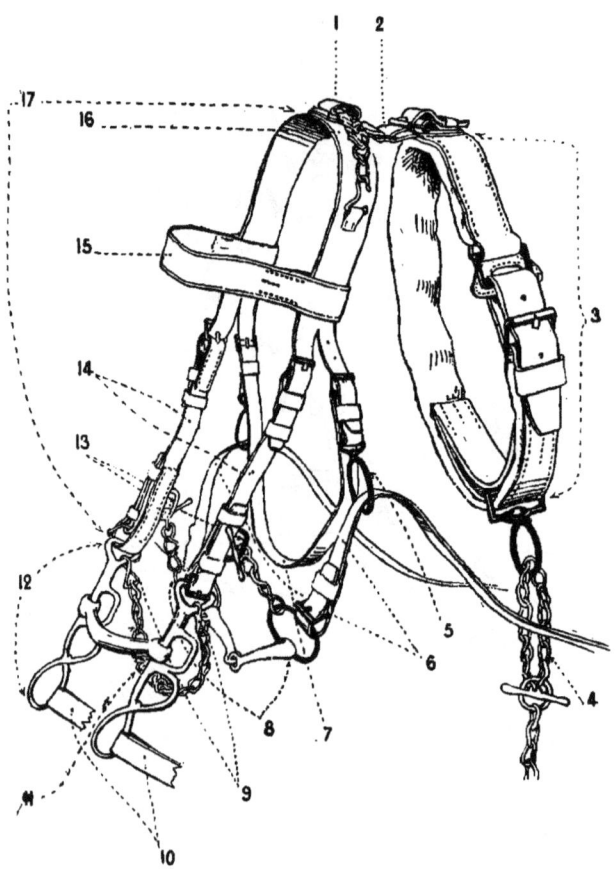

Head Harness or Bridle.
(French type 1874.)

Part Nos.
1. Crown piece. — Chape de dessus de tête.
2. Neck halter connecting strap. — Contre-sanglon.
3. Neck halter. — Collier d'attache.
4. Tether chain. — Longe en chaîne.
5. Oval rein support ring. — Panurge.
6. Snaffle rein. — Rênes de filet.
7. Throat latch. — Sous-gorge.
8. Snaffle bit. — Mors de filet.
9. Curb chain links (open and closed). — Crochets de gourmette.
10. Curb rein. — Rênes de bride.
11. Curb chain. — Gourmette.
12. Curb bit. — Mors de bride.
13. "D" Ring. — Dés.
14. Cheek strap. — Montants.
15. Brow band. — Frontal.
16. Spare curb chain. — Gourmette de rechange.
17. Head stall. — Têtière.

French Supply Caisson.

The French Supply Caisson (Caisson de Ravitaillement) allotted to Machine Gun companies comprises an ordinary limber chest type 1858 and a rear carriage chest of large capacity type 1909. The following accessories are carried and can be used as a guide for accessories to be carried in the four horse combat wagon furnished by the Quartermaster Department.

Ammunition.

8	Ammunition chests with strips (Rear chest). Caisses à munitions de l'arrière-train, cartouches sur bandes.	2304
	Cartridges in metal strips (Front chest). Cartouches sur bandes, en vrac dans l'avant-train.	7392
	Cartridges in metal strips (Rear chest). Cartouches sur bandes, en vrac dans l'arrière-train.	10752
		20448

Horse Equipment.

4 Blankets. — Couvertures de cheval (4).
2 Bridles, riding, fitted with curb bit, neck straps, and chain. — Brides de porteur avec mors à gourmette, sous-gorge et longe en chaîne (2).

2	Bridles, lead off horse, with neck strap and chain.	Brides de sous-verge avec sous-gorge et longe en chaîne (2).
4	Sets artillery harness complete.	Harnechement d'artillerie complet (4).
4	Nose-bags.	Musettes mangeoires (4).
2	Grooming bags.	Sacs de pansage (2).
2	Pair saddlebags, canvas.	Bissacs en toile (2).
2	Riding saddles.	Selles de porteur (2).
2	Harness saddles.	Sellettes (2).
4	Surcingles.	Sous-ventrières (4).
1	Horse rope (16 meters).	Corde à chevaux, de 16 mètres.
16	Mule shoes.	Fers à mulet (16).
1	Pkg. nails (160).	Clous à ferrer, paquet (160).
64	Frost nails.	Crampons (64).
2	Nail wrenches.	Clefs à pointe (2).
1	Tap wrench for horse shoes.	Clef à taraud.

Accessories.

	Camping Kit (Sledge hammer and 4 pickets).	Ustensile de campement (Masse de campement, et 4 piquets d'attache).
2	Round nose shovels (long handles).	Pelles rondes modèle 1862 (2).
2	Pick axes.	Pioches (2).
1	Axe hammer.	Hache à tête.
	Candles, 500 grammes.	Bougies 500 grammes.
	Large oil can, filled.	Burette de 90, garnie d'huile.
	Grease box.	Boîte à graisse, de campagne, modèle 1858.
	Oil can wrench model 1880.	Clef de bouchon de burette modèle 1880.
	Spare piston.	Piston de rechange.
1	No. 5 A Wheel.	Roue Nº 5 bis, de rechange pour voiturette.
1	Pair traces complete.	Traits d'attelage complets (paire).
1	Trace cover.	Étui de traits de rechange.
	Spare pole.	Timon de rechange.
	Linch pin and ring.	Esse à anneau de rechange.
	Folding lantern and case.	Lanterne pliante et étui.
6	Sheets of mica in portfolio.	Feuilles de mica dans portefeuille (6).
3	Padlocks.	Cadenas (3).
1	Padlock key.	Clef de cadenas.
1	Book (set of instructions).	Instruction sur le matériel.

Cartridges Carried on Light Carts.

M. G. Cart.
7 Boxes (Strips). Each box contains 12 strips of
  24 cartridges   2016
  (Each or 288 cartridges per box.)
1 Box (Belt) contains 1 belt of 250 cartridges . .   250

Ammunition Cart.
12 Boxes (Strips)   3456
2 Boxes (Belt)   500

               Total on carts   6222

Ammunition carried on French Caisson (Limber chest type 1858) cartridges   20448

Weight of Hotchkiss Equipment.

APPROXIMATE WEIGHT OF MISCELLANEOUS ITEMS

	Kgs.	Lbs.
Hotchkiss Machine Gun, model 1914	24.0	52.8
Tripod Mount, Omnibus type, model 1915	26.5	58.4
Tripod Mount, Hotchkiss model 1916	25.0	55.0
Hotchkiss Ammunition Case, loaded, with 12 strips (288 cart's.) model 1886 D (a. m.)	12.8	28.2
Same-empty	3.2	7.05
Hotchkiss Ammunition Case loaded with one belt 249 cartridges model 1886 D (a. m.)	12.0	26.4
Same-empty	4.0	8.8
Accessories and spare parts, including large and small pouch	9.5	24.6
Spare barrel in case	13.0	28.6
Spare barrel, without its case	10.6	23.8
Carts :		
Machine Gun Cart loaded	540.0	1188.0
Ammunition Cart loaded	380.0	836.0
Supply caisson :		
Caisson Limber Chest, model 1858 loaded, Cartridges model 1886 D (a. m.) and carrying tools	645.0	1419.0
Rear Carriage Chest, model 1909, loaded, Cartridges model 1886 D (a. m.) and carrying tools, horseshoe case, etc.	1075.0	2365.0
Total weight of the loaded caisson, with accessories and spare parts	1720.0	3784.0

General Description of the Hotchkiss Machine Gun Model 1914.

The Hotchkiss Machine Gun consists of a barrel attached to a receiver which incloses the firing, breech and feed mechanisms. The barrel differs from the ordinary rifle barrel only in that it is made heavier in order to withstand the vibrations and heating caused by prolonged fire. Below the barrel, parallel to it and connected with it by an orifice is the gas chamber which contains the front end of the piston. The cams on this piston operate the feed, firing and locking mechanisms.

When the piston is driven to the rear by the gas from the explosion of the cartridge, it is held at the end of its rearward movement by the sear engaging in a notch on the under side of the piston. When this sear is disengaged from the notch by pulling the trigger, the piston, being no longer held, is thrown forward to the first position by a return spring which was compressed during the rearward movement of the piston. If the trigger is held back and the sear kept out of the notch the piston does not stop at the end of its rearward movement, but will continue to move backward and forward as long as there is an uninterrupted feed of cartridges.

During the movement of the piston to the rear, the breech is opened, the empty shell extracted and ejected, and the strip is fed a certain distance through the feed box to the right.

During the forward movement of the piston a cartridge is pushed into the chamber, the breech block locked against the chamber, and the primer hit by the striker. The strip is fed through 1/12 of a turn of the feed wheel.

The cartridges are held either in a stiff metallic strip about 15 inches long, holding 24 cartridges, or in jointed metallic belts each holding 250 cartridges.

The loading is done by placing the strips or belts in the feed box one after the other. For transport the strips and belts are carried in ammunition boxes.

The belts are rolled up in a box which is placed along side of the gun during firing. To load, pass the end of the belt through the feed box, left to right. The belt will unroll automatically during firing.

The feed mechanism consists of a shaft carrying two wheels : one of these wheels is actuated by cams on the piston and is given an intermitten motion of rotation. The other wheel, which has the rotary motion at the same time, is the feed wheel proper and engages the strip on which it acts as a hook. Each forward and backward movement, i. e. a cycle of the piston places a cartridge opposite the chamber, ready to be pushed into the chamber by the breech block and struck by the striker as soon as the breech block is locked.

The machine gun has a handle block which is held in the left hand and a pistol grip which the firer grasps with the right hand.

As a rule two men operate the gun — one firing and one loading. However, one man can operate it alone in case of necessity.

Action of the Mechanism of the Hotchkiss Machine Gun Model 1914.

Starting with the breech closed.

For the first shot, pull the piston to the rear by means of the cocking piece which compresses the return spring.

During this movement the locking dog is raised by the unlocking slope on the piston. As soon as the locking dog is horizontal the breech block is drawn to the rear. The striker is withdrawn during the unlocking. At the end of the rearward movement the sear notch is slightly past the sear and the safety lug is bearing against the safety sear. Thus the piston is held back and the piece is ready to load. To load, the strip is introduced into the feed box (left to right) and pushed through as far as it will go. The strip presses down on the safety sear, disengaging it from the safety lug. The piston moves slightly forward until the sear is engaged in the sear notch. At the same time one tooth of the feed wheel engages the first opening of the strip and the first cartridge is ready to be pushed into the chamber. On pulling the trigger, the piston being free is thrown forward by the action of the return spring, carrying with it the breech block. The first cartridge, being in front of the chamber is partially lifted out of the strip by the stripping finger. The breech block bearing on the cartridge pushes the cartridge into the chamber and the claw of the extractor rides over the rim of the cartridge head. When the strip is exhausted it falls to the ground, and the safety sear which had been constantly held down is released, as soon as the last cartridge is fired. In spite of a pull on the trigger, the piston cannot move forward being held this time in the cocked position by the safety sear. The breech then remains open. As soon as a new strip is inserted in the feed box, it presses on the safety sear and disengages it from the safety lug. The piston is again free and automatic fire is resumed immediately.

The insertion of a strip into the feed box should be done by forcing it in as far as it will go with a steady pressure. No unnecessary force should be used. It is recommended that the strips never be hooked one to the other. Nor that they be made to follow each other without making a slight pause between each of them.

To Strip the Hotchkiss Machine Gun.

The firing mechanism must be down.

1. **Remove the feed box.** Withdraw the feed box locking pin to the rear. Withdraw the feed box to the left. (Tap both the feed box locking pin and the feed box lightly with the bronze hammer if necessary).
2. **To strip the feed box.** — Press on the forward end of the feed ratchet pin, turn the feed ratchet pawl until it is disengaged from the feed ratchet pin and withdraw it. Pull out the feed ratchet pin and the feed ratchet spring. Unseat the safety sear spring. Remove feed and feed ratchet wheels.
3. **Remove the handle block pin.** — Push the end of the return spring guide forward and pull the pin out.
4. **Remove the handle block.** — Pull it to the rear.
5. **Remove the return spring.** — Pull it to the rear.
6. **Remove the pistol grip.** — Pull it to the rear.
7. **Remove the trigger and sear.** — Pull the trigger to the rear and allow the sear to roll forward and fall out. Disengage the sear spring from the sear.
8. **Remove the piston and breech block.** — Pull the swan head to the rear until the piston is entirely out of the receiver.
9. **Disengage the breech block from the piston.** — Push the breech block to the rear until the ribs on the breech block lug can be disengaged from the forward end of the ribs inside the breech block.
10. **Remove the striker.** — Hold the breech block vertically with the locking dog open and shake the striker out.
11. **Remove the extractor.** — Insert the heel of the hand extractor in one of the coils of the extractor springs. Pull the spring forward and upward until the spring is unseated. Shake out the extractor.
12. **Remove the cocking piece.** — Pull it to the rear until the lugs on the forward end clear the rear end of the grooves on the side of the receiver.
13. **Remove the cocking piece spring latch.** — Raise the forward end of the spring and turn it to the side through the arc of 90 degrees and lift it off the cocking piece.
14. **Remove the ejector.** — Turn the toe 90 degrees outward and pull it out.
15. **Remove the gas cylinder.** — Unscrew the gas cylinder locking screw four (4) turns. Unscrew and remove the regulator. Unscrew the gas cylinder from the gas cylinder band turning it clockwise with the barrel wrench looking at it from the front. Should any force be required to turn it, tap the outer end of the wrench with a block of wood. Do not attempt to force it by pressure on the wrench.

16. **Remove the barrel.** — Cock the gun and turn the handle of the barrel lock to the rear until it engages out the stud on the side of the receiver. Apply the barrel wrench over the gas cylinder band. Turn counter clockwise, looking at it from the front, until the barrel stop on the right side of the barrel strikes the receiver, withdraw the barrel to the front. Should any force be required to turn the barrel do not exert any pressure on the wrench but tap the end of the wrench with a block of wood.

Note. — Many tripod legs and receivers are broken and strained by not observing above instruction.

To Assemble the Hotchkiss Machine Gun.

1. Insert the barrel in the front end of the receiver and turn the barrel clockwise, looking at it from the front, until the barrel stop mark on the barrel coincides with the barrel stop mark on the receiver. Turn the barrel lock handle as far to the front as it will go.

2. Screw the gas cylinder into the gas cylinder band as far as it will go and until the gas cylinder stop mark on the left side of the gas cylinder coincides with the stop mark on the gas cylinder band.

Note. — The gas cylinder must be turned counter clockwise, looking at it from the front. Screw in the gas cylinder locking screw.

3. Screw in the gas regulator. Set it at 3.

4. Assemble the cocking piece spring latch to the cocking piece. Reverse the operation of stripping.

5. Replace the cocking piece. — Insert the ribs on the lug on the forward end of the cocking piece in the grooves on the left side of the receiver and push the cocking piece as far forward as it will go.

6. Seat the ejector. — Reverse the operation of removing it from the receiver.

7. Insert the striker in the breech block.

8. Assemble the extractor and the extractor spring to the breech block. — Slip the spring over the spindle of the extractor. Seat the head of the extractor in the extractor housing. Hook the heel of the hand extractor in one of the coils of the spring. Pull forward and seat the spring.

9. Assemble the breech block and piston. — Insert the locking dog as far as it will go under the locking slope first making sure that the lug on the striker is in its proper recess in the piston. Engage the ribs on the breech block lug on top of the ribs inside the breech block. Push the breech block forward as far as it will go on the breech block lug.

10. Insert the piston and breech block in the receiver and push them as far forward as they will go.

11. Seat the sear spring on the sear and seat them in

the receiver. Hold the sear with the sear spring nearly vertical and pointing slightly to the rear. Insert the sear through the bottom of the receiver in front of the sear ribs and allow the trigger to roll forward.

12. Replace the pistol grip. — Engage the grooves on the pistol grip with the ribs in the bottom of the receiver and push the pistol grip forward.

13. Insert the return spring. — *Note.* — Care should be taken in seating the sear that the rear end of the sear spring does not ride up so as to interfere with the return spring. The trigger should be held forward until the pistol grip is seated.

14. Replace the handle block. — Slide it on to the receiver from the rear.

15. Insert the handle block pin. Push the end of the return spring guide forward.

16. Assemble the feed box. — Seat the safety sear spring on safety sear and seat them in the feed box. Seat the feed and feed ratchet wheel in the feed box. Place the feed ratchet pin spring on the feed ratchet pin. Insert the feed ratchet pin in the feed box pinning the safety sear and feed and feed ratchet wheels to the feed box. Seat the feed ratchet pawl in the feed box and turn it, locking it to the feed ratchet pin.

17. Replace the feed box. — Cock the piece. Insert the feed box in its grooves in the receiver from the left side, seating an oval tooth in each loading groove. Lock it in place by inserting the feed box locking pin from the rear.

18. Operate the mechanism by hand a few times. Do not leave the piece cocked.

TIMING TABLE.

The following table shows the action of the parts of the Hotchkiss Machine Gun during one cycle, i. e. one closing and opening of the breech. Starting with the piece cocked, strip inserted in the feed box and first cartridge in the strip presented in front of the breech block and ending with the sear engaged in the sear not h, strip in place and the second cartridge of the strip in front of the breech block.

Each half of the cycle is divided into three phases.

Closing Half.

1. From the time the sear is disengaged from the sear notch, until the locking dog begins to drop.

2. From the time the locking dog begins to drop until the breech block is locked against the end of the chamber.

3. From the time the breech block is locked against the chamber until the striker hits the primer.

Opening Half.

1. From the time the piston starts to the rear until the locking dog begins to rise.
2. From the time the locking dog begins to rise until it is horizontal.
3. From the time the locking dog is horizontal until the sear is engaged in the sear notch.

Tables.

Opening.

PART Nos.	PART.	1st PHASE.	2nd PHASE.	3rd PHASE.
33	Piston.	Travels to the rear.	Travels to the rear.	Travels to the rear.
75	Return spring.	Compressing.	Compressing.	Compressing.
37	Short cam.			Acts on one oval tooth of feed ratchet wheel turning it 1/12 of a turn.
38	Long cam.			
39	Striker lug.	Draws striker to rear.	Draws striker to rear.	Draws striker to rear.
41	Breech block lug.			Draws breech block to rear.
123	Unlocking slope.		Lifts locking dog to horizontal.	
45	Locking slope.			
49	Breech block.			Travels to rear carrying extractor and empty shell.
50	Locking dog.		Rising to horizontal.	Travels to rear on guide.

— 59 —

No.	Part				
56	Ejector.	Heel in rear groove. Toe on surface of breech block.	Heel in rear groove. Toe on surface of breech block.		Toe enters front groove and ejects empty shell. Heel leaves rear groove and rides on surface of breech block.
63	Feed ratchet wheel.				Makes 1/12 of a turn, turning feed wheel under action of short cam.
62	Feed wheel.	Holds strip so cartridge lies against breech block.	Holds strip so cartridge lies against breech block.		Makes 1/12 of a turn, feeding strip through feed box so as to lay cartridge in front of breech block.
70	Feed ratchet pawl.	Prevents feed ratchet wheel turning backward.	Prevents feed ratchet wheel turning backward.		Rides over one ratchet prevents feed ratchet wheel turning backward.
124	Loading grooves.	Travels to rear holding an oval tooth. Prevents feed ratchet wheel turning.	Travels to rear holding an oval tooth. Prevents feed ratchet wheel turning.	Travels to rear.	
65	Safety sear.	Held down by strip.	Held down by strip.		Held down by strip until last cartridge is fired. Then strip is ejected and safety sear rises and blocks forward motion of piston.

Closing.

Part Nos.	Part.	1st Phase.	2nd Phase.	3rd Phase.
33	Piston.	Travels forward.	Travels forward.	Travels forward.
75	Return spring.	Elongating.	Elongating.	Elongating.
37	Short cam.			
38	Long cam.	Acts on one oval tooth turning feed ratchet wheel 1/12 of a turn.		
39	Striker lug			
41	Breech block lug.	Travels forward.	Travels forward.	Travels forward pushing striker.
123	Unlocking slope.			
45	Locking slope.	Travels forward pushing locking dog and breech block.	Travels forward pushing down locking dog.	Holds down locking dog.
49	Breech block.	Moves forward pushing cartridge out of strip and seats cartridge in chamber.	Supports cartridge in chamber. Breech block stops against face of chamber. Extractor claw rides over cartridge rim.	Supports cartridge in chamber.

No.	Part			
50	Locking dog.	Moves forward on guide ribs.	Drops down in locked position under action of locking slope.	Holds breech block against face of chamber.
56	Ejector.	Toe runs out of front groove onto surface of breech block. Heel enters rear groove from surface of breech block.	Heel runs in rear groove. Toe on surface of breech block.	Heel runs in rear groove. Toe on surface of breech block.
63	Feed ratchet wheel.	Turned 1/12 of a turn by action of long cam on an oval tooth turning feed wheel.		
62	Feed wheel.	Turned 1/12 of a turn feeding strip through feed box so as to lay a cartridge against the breech block.	Holds strip so cartridge lies against breech block.	Holds strip so cartridge lies against breech block.
70	Feed ratchet pawl.	Rides over one ratchet prevents feed ratchet wheel turning backward.	Prevents feed ratchet wheel turning backward.	Prevents feed ratchet wheel turning backward.
124	Loading grooves.	Travels forward. Prevents feed ratchet wheel turning backward after it is turned.	Travels forward. Prevents feed ratchet wheel turning backward.	Travels forward. Prevents feed ratchet wheel turning backward.
65	Safety sear.	Held down by strip.	Held down by strip.	Held down by strip.

Precautions to be Taken *Before* Firing Hotchkiss Machine Gun.

(*a*) See that the barrel locking key is at forward closed position.
(*b*) Cock the gun.
(*c*) Pass cleaning rod through the bore.
(*d*) See that gas regulator on all available barrels is set for normal gas regulation (3 to 4). See note. Gas Regulator.
(*e*) Oil mechanism moderately — not necessary to flood piece.
(*f*) Test action of mechanism by opening and closing breech rapidly several times.
(*g*) Attach flash arrestor if it is to be used.
(*h*) Attach elevating and traversing blocks if necessary.
(*i*) Verify sight setting and aim.

Gas Regulator.

NOTE. — To obtain the proper regulator setting remove the gas regulator entirely and fire one or two shots to clear the orifice on all new barrels. Set the gas regulator at 4.0 and fire a single shot. If the gun shows symptoms of insufficient gas screw regulator down several turns, and try again. Repeat until the gun shows no further symptoms of insufficient gas. Then screw regulator down two more turns to insure positive action. This setting should be recorded and the gun habitually left at this reading.

Results of insufficient gas.
  1. Failure to eject.
  2. Uncontrolled automatic fire.

Results of too much gas.
  1. Excessive speed causing pounding.
  2. Extractor tears rim of cartridge.
  3. Ejector marks or cuts through rim of cartridge.

Precautions to be Taken *During* Firing.

(*a*) During firing press firmly on the trigger so that the sear will work freely.
(*b*) Never try to make the strips follow each other without interruption; on the contrary, make a short pause after each strip.
(*c*) In case of a stoppage with a loaded cartridge inserted in the chamber and the barrel at a high temperature, it is expedient to allow the barrel to cool if the stoppage

cannot be corrected within 30 seconds. When searching for the trouble when the barrel is hot do not look into the ejector opening if there is a loaded cartridge in the chamber.

(d) Look at the barrel lock frequently to see that it does not jar out of its position.

(e) The bore cleaning rod should be run through the bore after every 200 or 300 rounds.

(f) Take advantage of every opportunity to clean and oil the mechanism.

(g) The barrel should be cooled after every 500 rounds during firing. This may be done by lowering the muzzle of the barrel into a bucket of water, wrapping the barrel with wet rags or pouring water over the barrel.

Precautions to be Taken *After* Firing.

(a) Unload and clear the piece. Pull back as far as possible on the cocking piece and pull out the strip. Work the mechanism twice to be sure that there are no cartridges in the chamber.

(b) Clean all parts of the gun while still warm. This makes the work much easier than waiting for even ten or fifteen minutes as the parts can all be cleaned much easier when warm than when cool. (See Chapter on "Care of the Gun".)

Loading the Hotchkiss Machine Gun.
"Standing or Kneeling".

Face squarely in front of the mouth of the feed box, left foot slightly in advance, hold the strip, cartridge side up, with the left hand on left side of strip near forward end (5th cartridge) fingers under the strip, thumb passing over the bullets and pressing down upon the cartridge cases near the base of the cartridges; the right hand holding the strip on the right side near the outer end, fingers under the strip, thumb on top. Place the forward end of the strip on the floor of the feed box the strip entering the box in a horizontal plane, the rear end upward at an angle of about 15 degrees. Push the strip home with an easy and quick movement of the right hand.

The strip is held by the hands in a similar manner from the kneeling position.

This method of loading requires the loader to place himself opposite the feed box-his proper place-and the strip enters the box properly. The position and fingers of the left hand insures the strip passing under the front feed guides, while the pressure of the left thumb assists the strip under the stripping finger.

After a little practice this method easily becomes the most rapid, especially when a great many strips have to be loaded under stress of action, as there are practically no jams from improper entering of feed strips, no "Columbus Jams". The method is applicable in machine gun emplacements.

To Unload the Hotchkiss Machine Gun.

To unload or to withdraw partially extended feed strip: Release the feed pawl from the ratchet of feed ratchet wheel by pulling cocking handle to rear as far as possible. The feed wheel is then free to turn backwards and the strip is withdrawn (to the left).

To Let Down Mechanism.

Piece cocked and strip withdrawn:
Lift the safety sear off safety sear lug. Pull the trigger and ease down the mechanism by holding back on the cocking piece handle.

Jams, Malfunctions and Stoppages.

The most frequent cause of malfunctions of the Hotchkiss Machine Gun is the feeding of the cartridges. To minimize malfunctions due to this cause it is necessary to pay special attention to the proper positioning of the cartridges in the belt and the proper insertion of the strips and belts in the gun. In any mechanism with as many requirements and limitations as a machine gun there are necessarily a number of things that may cause trouble. The more common of these causes are listed in the following table.

I. **Improper manipulation.**
(a) Strip or belt improperly loaded (not lined up).
(b) Gun improperly loaded (strip not pushed entirely home).
(c) Safety sear left out in assembling.
(d) Dirt in chamber.
(e) Clogged or partially clogged gas port.
(f) Failure to oil mechanism.

II. **Break:**
(a) Striker.
(b) Extractor.
(c) Extractor spring.
(d) Return spring.

(e) Ejector.
(f) Feed ratchet pin spring.

III. Worn or deformed parts.
(a) Short striker.
(b) Weak return spring.
(c) Excessive head space causing ruptured cartridges.
(d) Stripping finger.
(e) Weak extractor spring.

IV. Defective ammunition.
(a) Misfire.
(b) Battered or deformed ammunition.
(c) Primer caps coming off.

The malfunctions listed above cause the breech mechanism to stop in certain positions. The causes of the various stoppages together with the immediate action to be taken are listed below.

1st position. — Breech block all way home.
Probable cause :
A. Misfire. Defective ammunition.
B. Failure to fire.
    1. Short or broken striker.
    2. Weak return spring.
    3. Excessive friction.
    4. Barrel assembled one thread out too far.
C. Failure to feed :
    1. Feed box locking pin out.
    2. Defective feed ratchet pawl or spring.
    3. Defective feed wheel.
    4. Empty space in feed strip.
    5. Feed strip improperly entered.
D. Gun fires but fails to recoil :
    1. Clogged gas port.
    2. Gas regulator missing.
E. Mechanism not locked
    1. Foreign substance in chamber.
    2. Loose primer in mechanism.

Immediate action.

Count five seconds to allow for hangfire, then cock the gun and continue firing. If the trouble recurs cock the gun and examine the ejected cartridge. If the primer has been struck a good blow its a misfire. If the primer has been struck a light blow or none at all the probable cause is (B) or (E). In case the chamber is empty the cause is (C). If an empty shell is ejected the probable cause is (D). Make the necessary repairs and continue firing.

In case of failure to feed due to defective feed mechanism, the gun may be fed by hand by simply pressing the feed strip through the feed opening. Even with the feed box entirely removed, automatic fire can be continued until the pressure on the feed strip is released. Make the necessary repairs at the first opportunity.

2nd position. — Face of breech block near front end of ejection opening.

Probable cause :
 A. Ruptured cartridge (Excessive headspace).
 B. Battered cartridge.

Immediate action.

Pull back cocking handle and attempt to continue the fire. If the gun jams again, cock the gun and examine the ejected cartridge. If it has the front part of a ruptured cartridge telescoped onto it continue firing. If the ejected cartridge shows the imprint of ruptured shell around its shoulder, clear the chamber with a defective cartridge extractor, and continue firing. If the ejected cartridge is battered glance at the cartridge in the feed strip. If these are in good condition, continue firing.

In case of ruptured cartridges, replace the breech block. If trouble recurs change barrels. If these fail, the receiver is probably strained or the recoil blocks are worn and the gun will have to be turned in for repairs.

3rd position. — Face of breech block half way in ejection opening.

Probable cause :
 A. Failure to extract.
  1. Weak or broken extractor spring.
  2. Worn or chipped extractor claw.
  3. Worn or broken shoulder on breech block.
 B. Failure to eject.
  1. Broken or missing ejector.
  2. Insufficient gas.

Immediate action.

Cock gun, remove damaged cartridges from the feed way and chamber and continue firing.

If the trouble recurs, glance in ejection opening. If the point of live cartridge is jammed against the base of empty shell in the chamber, remove the breech block and examine for faulty extraction.

If two cartridges, one live and one empty are jammed in the feed way due to a failure to eject, look at ejector. If this is in place, screw down the gas regulator a few turns. If the trouble still persists, resize the feed strips at the first opportunity.

Uncontrolled automatic fire.

Probable cause :
 A. Insufficient gas.
 B. Worn or broken sear or sear spring.
 C. Sear binds on receiver.

Immediate action.

On the firing line allow the feed strip to fire through. Then screw down the gas regulator a few turns. If this does not correct the trouble examine and repair the trigger mechanism at the first opportunity.

Uncontrolled automatic fire may occur in a critical situation when a metal belt is being used or when it is desired to stop firing in the middle of a feed strip. In this case fire may be controlled by pulling back the cocking handle which stops the piston on its forward movement. Hold the piston back in the cocked position until it is desired to reopen fire or until the gun is unloaded. Firing is re-opened by letting go of the cocking handle.

Care of the Machine Gun.

General Considerations.

The machine gun should be kept in perfect condition to insure its maximum usefulness. All parts of the gun, especially those subject to friction, should be covered with a thin coat of oil. A light oil is preferable. Polish should never be used on either the steel or bronze parts. When the gun is in action every cessation of fire should be taken as an opportunity to clean the bore and mechanism as far as possible. As a rule, after every 250 rounds the bore should have an oiled brush or rag run through it. When the firing is over, the gun should be stripped and every part cleaned thoroughly. If possible this should be done while the gun is still warm.

Rust Prevention.

The gun, as a fine piece of machinery, should never be allowed to rust. When in daily use, it should be covered with a very light film of oil, applied with a piece of soft cloth or waste. After any handling of the gun, as at drills, the whole gun should be gone over, part by part, wiped dry if there is moisture on it and then lightly oiled as described. Special care must be taken if the gun has been wet by rain or otherwise. In very dry climates where the dust is bad, it may be possible and even desirable, to keep the gun thoroughly dry and not to oil it against rust, but in this case, the utmost vigilance must be exercised to see that the gun is dry and clean before being put away. Sweaty hands on a dry or lightly oiled gun means rust later on.

One of the most important constituents of powder gas is water vapor. This necessitates special care to prevent rusting of the mechanism after firing. In a machine gun, the powder gas emerges from the breech with considerable force and permeates the whole breech mechanism This makes it necessary to pay special attention to small springs and other hidden parts which, because they are small and apparently well protected, are likely to be overlooked and neglected in cleaning the gun after firing.

If the gun is to be stored or packed for shipment, it should be thoroughly cleaned and given a light coat of cosmic. This should be applied to all parts, moving and otherwise, inside and outside of the gun. The cosmic can be warmed until liquid, and applied with a grease brush. A thin coat protects quite as well as a thick one and is much easier to remove later on.

The best medium for removing cosmic and other greases is gasoline. Apply it freely with a grease brush or place the part in gasoline and scrub with a brush or a cloth. Smoking or open lights must never be permitted near while working with gasoline as it is highly inflammable. After cleaning a part with gasoline, it should be rubbed off with a dry rag to remove the gasoline residue and then lightly rubbed over with an oily rag.

Cleaning of the Gun.

(a) The bore. The gunner should, as part of his daily routine, wipe out the bore of the barrel and also the spare barrel. The bores should then be lightly oiled so that the rifling can be clearly seen. After firing, the bore of the gun is covered with fouling. This is of two kinds, a black deposit covering the entire bore, caused by the burning powder and removable with hot sal soda solution and rags, and a metallic fouling, caused by particles of the metal jacket of the bullet adhering to the barrel and which can be best removed by ammonia solution. The firing of merely a few shots will produce enough fouling to necessitate a thorough cleaning of the bore. After each 500 rounds the barrel should be cooled by putting wet rags upon it or tipping the muzzle forward into a bucket of water.

(b) The gas port in the barrel and gas cylinder should be cleaned.

(c) The gas cylinder must be removed from the gas cylinder band to be cleaned. It is cleaned with the scraper and gas cylinder cleaning brush and kept dry. The gas regulator, piston, sleeve and threads should be oiled.

(d) The inside of the receiver should be cleared of dirt and brass filings by using rags and a stick. It should be oiled, particularly the guide ribs and grooves.

(e) The carbon on the head of the piston and on the gas regulator piston should be cleaned off by friction with the scraper or kerosene or gasoline.

(f) The traversing head, tripod and flash arrestor must be kept cleaned and oiled, particularly the joints and threads.

(g) The extra parts in the spare part case must be kept cleaned and oiled.

Inspection After Cleaning.

Whenever the guns are cleaned, particularly after firing, they will, before being put away, be thoroughly inspected by an officer who will make certain that it has been properly cleaned, oiled and adjusted. The mechanism should be operated several times to insure proper functioning. A daily record must be kept of the lot of ammunition used, the number of rounds fired from each barrel and the gun adjustments. Note will be made of any troubles or stoppages and how they were remedied. This daily performance record should be kept with the gun at all times if possible.

Testing the Chamber.

Barrels that have fired 14.000 rounds should never be used for overhead fire. The chamber should be tested from time to time, especially if shells rupture during firing. The method is to insert the chamber gauge in the chamber and lower the mechanism slowly by hand. If the mechanism goes completely forward and the locking dog locks, the chamber is worn and the barrel should be sent to the repair shop for reconstruction.

Protection against gas attacks.

The best protection against gas is a good coat of oil. Occasional short bursts of fire will lessen the chance of guns jamming from the action of the gas. After a gas attack the gun must be cleaned and oiled at once, and at the first opportunity it should be stripped and all working parts cleaned in boiling water containing a little soda.

The effects of corrosion on the ammunition are even more serious than upon the gun. Ammunition should be kept in a box the joints of which can be made tight by inserting strips of cloth. All ammunition on hand during a gas attack should be cleaned and used at the first opportunity.

www.ingramcontent.com/pod-product-compliance
Lightning Source LLC
Chambersburg PA
CBHW060215050426
42446CB00013B/3075